GEORDIE'S WAR

ALAN RICHARDSON

© Alan Richardson, 2013
Foreword © Sting, 2013

First published in Great Britain in 2013 by Skylight Press,
210 Brooklyn Road, Cheltenham, Glos GL51 8EA

All rights reserved. Except for the quotation of short passages for the purposes of criticism and review, no part of this publication may be reproduced, stored in a retrieval system or transmitted, in any form or by any means, electronic, mechanical, photocopying, recording or otherwise, without the prior consent of the copyright holder and publisher.

Alan Richardson has asserted his right to be identified as the author of this work.

Designed and typeset by Rebsie Fairholm
Publisher: Daniel Staniforth

www.skylightpress.co.uk

Printed and bound in Great Britain by Lightning Source, Milton Keynes.
Text set in LTC Italian Oldstyle. Titles set in Chancellor, a font by Pintassilgo Prints.

British Library Cataloguing in Publication Data:
A catalogue record for this book is available from the British Library.

ISBN 978-1-908011-74-9

To
George Matthew Richardson, M.M. & Bar
who held the line and came through
for all of us.
And to all Tommies everywhere...

CONTENTS

Acknowledgements	7
Foreword	9
Introduction	11
Dad's Watch	13
Into No Man's Land	20
Over the Top and Far Below	32
Ashington, and other Battlefields	40
Behind the Lines	68
The Naming of the Parts	78
Getting Stuck In	94
Strangers in a Strange Land	113
Further Over the Top	129
Giving a Push	151
Keeping Watch	164
Books to Read	172
Appendix 1	173
Appendix 2	174
Appendix 3	175

ACKNOWLEDGEMENTS

A great number of people have helped me in all sorts of ways.

Primarily my wife Margaret who, for months, spent every night in bed not just with me but with the 6$^{th.}$ & 13th Battalions of the Northumberland Fusiliers.

Capt. M. G. Straker, Chester Potts and Graham Heron of the Royal Regiment of Fusiliers. Katherine Philips of the Collections Enquiry Service, Imperial War Museum.

Michael Geary and staff of the Northumberland Archives at Woodhorn.

Bill Brabban, Nicola Frater and Lesley Frater of the Research Service at the excellent The Fusiliers Museum of Northumberland for their painstaking research involving the bewildering Medal Cards and other recondite puzzles.

Graham Stewart, the Greatest Living Englishman, for his painstaking work in cyber-space on behalf of me, a complete stranger.

Matthew Lucas for some nifty insights.

Steve Oram and David Seymour of the Western Front Association.

Sting, for his encouragement right from the beginning, when he set the Fusiliers marching through my head.

Then there is family: Cousins Jan and Peter Richardson, Margaret Mudge, Sheila Bird and Shirley Marshall, all of whom preserved enough of our grandad to do him proud.

With especial mention to 'Finally Found Cousin Bill Richardson' for all those things on all levels that have proved so precious.

And *then* there is Tony McCarroll and my sister Pat, without whose wisdom, memory and sheer lovingness none of this would have been possible.

Which necessarily brings in our Dad, George Matthew Richardson (1913-1991) who was the *real* hero in the eyes of me and Pat.

FOREWORD

BY STING

I'VE had a somewhat mawkish fascination for the so called 'Great War' since I was very young. My house was right opposite the Memorial Hall in Wallsend, and the sculpted bronze soldiers with their upturned rifles flanking the names of the town's fallen had a profound and lasting effect on me. I've read voraciously on the subject all my life, and it feels like more than just a strong connection. Perhaps, as Alan Richardson suggests in this quirky book, the generation that grew up after 1918 suffered the aftershocks of this War often without realising it. Who knows what anxieties and suppressed torments were passed down to the children which followed them.

It must have been a massive and unprecedented psychic event for the survivors and the families and the communities of the fallen when there were 60,000 British casualties before lunch on the first day of the Somme Offensive. Staggering!

Those who survived those monstrous battles and endless bloodbaths must have become inured to their feelings, or at least unable to express them in a coherent fashion. And I suspect there are still traces of this disconnect haunting us today, a century later.

One of the finest books on those years is Adam Hochschild's *To End All Wars*, written from the perspective of those who fought against it, the conscientious objectors who suffered enormously for their convictions. He regarded the War as a tragedy of mass psychosis, aided by rabid propaganda and misplaced nationalism. Personally I've always suspected it was a war cynically manufactured by the ruling elite to rid both sides of the potential for a Bolshevik revolution in western Europe.

Many years ago I had a long pub conversation with a veteran of the trenches. He was a card carrying Communist till the day he died. The clinching event for him was taking over a German trench and finding Blue Circle cement bags. To him, this was all the proof he needed that the capitalists who ran the war valued profits over patriotism.

While Hochschild analyses the global factors, *Geordie's War* looks at it from the (often bewildered but always determined) viewpoint of the ordinary Tommy. Richardson writes about his almost-forgotten grandfather in a way that makes him ours too, a kind of Everyman figure, and skilfully evokes his exploding world both at home in Northumberland and amid the carnage of Flanders.

We follow Wor Geordie, as he is called, every step of the way from behind the bar in the Grand Hotel in Ashington to the unimaginable slaughter in the mud of the Western Front, experiencing his huge tragedies and tiny victories. Not only does he show us what an ordinary fella might have experienced in those extraordinary times, he seeks to answer the question *Why?* at least to his own satisfaction. Although the author describes his book as something of a Plain Man's Guide to the Great War, it is more than that.

Under the deceptively simple prose and conversational tone, Richardson crafts another level of insight which shows how the Somme Offensive resonated within his own soul a century later. Tensions were passed down from his war hero grandfather, through his father, and into his own childhood, thus family conflicts became almost analogues or metaphors of the Great War itself. "We all dig trenches of differing kinds as we fight our own wars within our families," he writes – and there are plenty of troubled folk who would agree with that.

The book is never less than informative, with unexpected insights. At times it is extremely funny. By understanding the mechanism of his Dad's broken watch and then getting it repaired, as described in the moving opening chapter, he shapes the history of his grandfather, bonds with the spirit of his late father, learns to avoid minefields, re-unites his family and finds peace for his own future. And teaches us a helluva lot about the Northumberland Fusiliers...

Sting
Lake House
Wiltshire

INTRODUCTION

This is the story of one man who served throughout the Great War, at the very front of the Fronts in the most brutal battles in history, and achieved that most astonishing feat of all – he survived. His name was George Matthew Richardson. He won the Military Medal and Bar and was nominated for the Distinguished Conduct Medal, yet was completely forgotten by his country, his clan, his home town and – almost – his own family.

He was my grandfather, and yet we, his grandchildren, knew almost nothing about him. Nor did he ever talk much about the war to his own many children.

After a century of familial and national disinterest I became determined to find out how and why a very ordinary man was plucked from his job as a barman in the coal-mining town of Ashington in Northumberland to serve with distinction amid the slaughter of the Western Front. I wanted to find out why he joined up, how he was trained, what his regiment was like and his daily life therein, how he coped with the appalling conditions and unbelievable casualty rates suffered by the British Tommy. I also wanted to understand why he, and his mates, didn't just drop their rifles en masse and make their own ways home.

This is not meant as a scholarly analysis but more as a sort of Plain Man's Guide to the Great War. I've tried to provide a way for us to look at those dreadful years through the eyes of a common man who, apparently without history, proved to be very uncommon indeed. Which is the case with all 'common' men and women everywhere.

It is also something of a meditation on the more subtle personal wars that can go on between the generations, and the nature of what I might call 'Dadness', and how my grandfather's character and experience in the trenches of Flanders left echoes within my own psyche, 100 years later. In fact I think we all dig trenches of differing kinds as we fight our own wars within our families. Sometimes we spend our lives hiding in them, ducking down, terrified of having to face our biggest fears in that No Man's Land that can exist between ourselves and our parents, siblings or compatriots.

There are lots of things I still don't know about my grandfather and never will, but a century after he first went into battle near Ypres, he has taught me how to climb from that trench.

I've used my grandfather as a sort of avatar, as they seem to call it nowadays: a vehicle by which we can all try and understand those nightmare times between 1914 and 1918 when a whole generation was lost. Although this is called *Geordie's War* it could also be called *Geordies' War* in that it tells the tale of a tribe of ordinary folk with whom we can all identify whether we're Geordies, Scousers, Jocks or even part of the Cockney Mafia.

If I've got anything dreadfully wrong then readers are welcome to write to me c/o the publisher and I will try to put it right in any future edition.

Alan Richardson
Wiltshire

1

DAD'S WATCH

My Dad, a bent and battered old Northumbrian miner, had a pocket watch. It had been given to him by his Dad, and he regarded it as the only really valuable item he had ever owned.

The main spring was broken. He couldn't afford to get it fixed. Nor did he trust the watch repairers up in Ashington: he was convinced they would steal both the jewels in the watch's movements and the solid gold plate within the back case. He also kept it well hidden from Mam. I think he had a point.

On the few occasions when he showed it to me, and opened the case to reveal the loose glass and wonky face, it was as though all the hopes he had ever had for family, peace and achievement floated out, like mist, softening and bewildering his features. When the mist faded there was a brief frown, as he must have realised how broken his life was, and always had been. His own main spring had rusted and snapped long ago; his jewels certainly stolen and thrown away down a pit.

I knew the inscription well enough:

> Presented to
> Pte G.M. Richardson
> M.M. & Bar
> 13th Batt. N. Fusiliers
> by the
> Public of Ashington
> 22nd June 1917

I never met my grandad. He died in 1944, seven years before I was born. What little I knew about him and his whole family was filtered through the venom of my mother, who regarded all Richardsons as useless, hardly human, and used the witch-powers of The Mam to smoor the double helix of my DNA with her thick and sticky family bile, determined that nothing of me, her precious son, would connect in *that* direction.

The watch meant nothing to me. I was fairly wealthy, living in the Royal Crescent in posh Bath, one foot in America and one here. I earned decent money, had a good car, holidayed in France whenever I could. What attraction would a piece of polished scrap metal hold for me?

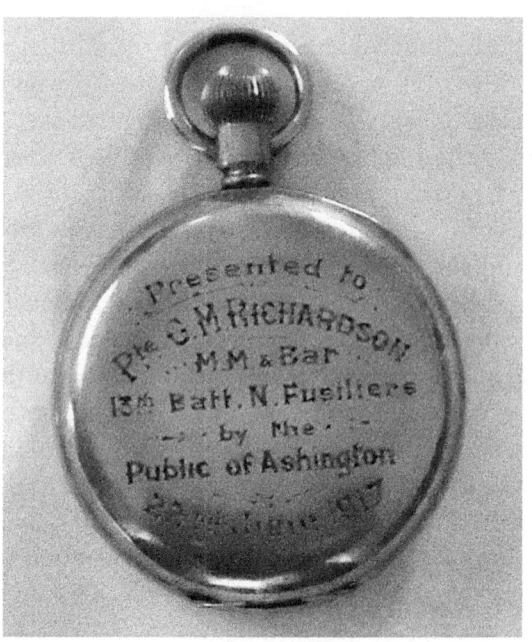

The Mam was gone, but here was my Dad now, being embarrassing as Dads invariably are. I had taken him to the upstairs restaurant of Evan's Fish & Chip Shop in Bath, which existed then in Abbey Green, a place of plastic chandeliers, tatty chairs, wobbly tables and the desultory service of the bored waitresses in their faded black outfits. He had entered with amazement, looking around at the mock (very mock) Regency décor and the free sachets of ketchup and tartare sauce and declared it be – and he paused on the word – an Emporium. And the way he said it, wide-eyed, it was clearly the Buckingham Palace of chippies, and he spoke to the youngsters who served him as if they were members of the lower aristocracy. God he annoyed me.

Then he took on a curious intensity, like you might see on the archbishop's face when he puts the crown on the new king's head.

"Ah want ye tae have this watch," he told me softly, keeping it shielded from the girl who brought the two plates of steaming cod and chips, as if she might glean its secrets. "Ah want ye tae look after it, nivver sell it, or give it tae anybody stupid."

I paused. Aware that this was a crucial moment in our fraught and fractured relationship, but not sure where I could find a splint to support the breaks.

"Here son, tayk it," he said, covering the watch in his big scarred fists, waiting for me to cup my girlie little hands and receive it.

I've thought of those hands many times in the decades since. His fingers were large and scarred, the nails always to the quick. He lost the tip of one in an accident down the Pit, as the coal mines were called up there, and with the compensation we had a week's holiday at Butlins Holiday Camp, in Ayr. Whenever I think of him I think of those hands, and a fragment of someone's poem always rises in my mind: 'Hands like shovels and great big heart'; and I kick myself anew for the grace I failed to show him.

"Tayk it," he insisted, and there was an edge of pleading in his voice.

But I had a quick sense of fear. Sometimes, Dad seemed to know things. I wondered if he'd had intimations of his own mortality, and wanted to pass this on while he still had a chance. For myself, I was often freakish enough to see life in terms of omens, patterns and synchronicities, and so instantly created the story within myself that when he passed this watch onto me, he would go home and die.

He annoyed me, he embarrassed me. We had spent so many years entangled in the barbed wires of family conflict but he was still my silver-haired dopey old Dad and I loved him stupidly if silently, and I didn't want him to go just yet.

"Ner Dad," I said, slipping back into the Geordie with which he was comfortable, and which I hadn't really spoken for years except when back in Ashington, in case the hard lads up there thought I was a poof.

His face fell.

"Lissen Dad, there's plenty of time left for that. Ye doan't need ter give it yet."

He looked at me sharply. Perhaps he was aware that, sometimes, I too knew things and hoped that I was speaking out of foresight rather than diffidence. He put the watch back into a little grey plastic purse and zipped its secrets away for another few years.

"So what did grandad do tae win his medals?"

He pursed his lips, frowned, looked at his plate. His relationship with his father, apparently, had been as awkward as mine had been with him. "He once said a Prussian nearly got him. Ah think he was in the machine-gun corps. An' later he became a stretcher bearer. That's aboot aall he would say."

We ate in silence for a little while, and our chips were sprinkled with our own guilt along with salt and pepper. I had never asked what Dad had done as a coal miner; I deliberately never showed any interest in his life and work, and spent years ignoring him. He had done exactly the same with his dad.

We finished our meal, wading through our conversation as if in deep mud, while things seemed to explode in the air around us like the German whizz-bangs of the Great War, and we kept our heads ducked below the parapet of stilted observations.

Although I paid by credit card (which he'd never seen before) he left the waitress a 50 pence tip, which I thought was both unnecessary and ridiculously large, though I said nothing and gave an exasperated shrug.

"That waz the best meal Ah've ivver had, son" he said as we clumped down the stairs and into the sunlight.

Ten years later I visited him in hospital, in Ashington. It was November. I don't recall the actual date but in our terms it was certainly Armistice Day, when the cannons had stopped and the earth no longer shook. I fancy it might have been the same ward where, 30 years before, he'd held up his ruined and bandaged finger, stained with blood and dripping with £60 worth of compensation and announced proudly: "We'll get a holiday oot o' this!"

The curtains around the bed were pulled back. The sun poured through the window and made him look very grey, and caused him to shade his eyes. He was sitting up. The two young Philippino nurses were straightening his sheets, and struggling with his accent. But he spoke to them as if they were members of the lower aristocracy at least, and I got it at last.

By then of course I had learned the painful truth behind Mark Twain's words: 'When I was a boy of 14, my father was so ignorant

I could hardly stand to have the old man around. But when I got to be 21, I was astonished at how much the old man had learned in seven years.' Except I was a lot older than Twain when I got to these crucial Damascene moments on the road to understanding The Dad.

"Ah want ye tae have the watch, son," he whispered, as if the girls might hear and act upon the information. He told me where it was hidden, in the back of a drawer at his home, in a little plastic purse wrapped in a hanky.

I nodded, he smiled with relief. "But divvn't pass it on tae anybody stupid, mind. It's precious, that. Sivventeen jewels an' a gold plate."

"It's far more precious than that, Dad. It's priceless."

He nodded. The effort seemed to exhaust him.

We both had the same knowing; we could see where things were heading. By this time I had children of my own – two girls, with two more to come, though he never lived to see the latter. Becoming a dopey and irritating old Dad myself was a sure-fire way of enabling me to see all the jewels he had, and the gold that was folded within, despite the power of The Mam.

I put my hand on his and he gave me a strange look, almost of surprise. It was the first time I had ever done that. It took me a while to realise where I had seen that expression before. It was on the faces of my children when they were being shy.

He was shy of me, simple as that. Probably always had been. It was not that, all along, he had been a difficult, all-powerful and enormously complex older being doing thoughtless things to hapless young me. He had just been a little boy inside, as bewildered by life as the rest of us, making all the same mistakes, and never quite knowing how to make his own life work, never mind ours.

I sat on the edge of his bed, on the edge of his life. I realised that, as long as he lived, I had always had the sense that no matter how bleak things were I could always go back home and he'd give me a few shillings pocket money and sweeties, stoke up the fire and keep me warm, dry and safe. I was 40 when he finally died, but there was always that absurd sense of safety that buoyed me in the later years when *I* wasn't well off, and didn't live in the Royal Crescent, and couldn't even afford a holiday as far as Wor Gate.

There were no whizz-bangs flying around our heads now. The fighting was all done. We were not struggling on barbed wire, nor trapped in mud, but walking slowly back from No Mans Land toward a safer place, with our arms around each other's shoulders.

This time I asked him about his family, and learned about his two brothers and four sisters, one of whom died in infancy. I wrote the names down on a paper napkin by the side of his bed, being careful not to tear the soft material with the biro, slightly guilty that I was almost insulting his memories by not immediately finding a proper piece of paper.

I folded it into a triangle, and put it in my shirt pocket.

"Bye son," he said when I left. "Divvn't forget the watch…"

My life went through many Wars in the years after he first offered it to me in that Emporium. I can't complain about the wounds I got along the way, or crow about the victories. I suppose a turning point came when I was walking down the High Street in Glastonbury and saw a Psychic Fayre advertised.

The hall was full of little stalls, most of them made from the fold-out paste tables that people use at car boot sales. It seemed like a refuge for ageing hippies, and smelled strongly of joss sticks.

One woman, advertising herself as an Internationally Renowned Psychic, offered readings for a pound a minute. I think she was from Canada. I have a tendency to believe everything I read in terms of advertising, which is why my wife Margaret keeps any gadget catalogue out of sight. If this woman said in bold print that she was an Internationally Renowned Psychic then it must be true. The woman was large, wore some sort of purpley kaftan thing with suns and moons running over her breasts, had a torrent of necklaces and silver rings on many fingers.

"Here ye go," I offered breezily. "Here's a fiver. What can you see?" I said, thinking I couldn't be done for a fiver.

She sat quietly, and looked at me with bemusement.

"I've got your Dad here," she said, without preamble, before I'd even spent as much as 20 pence.

I went quiet. I hadn't expected that. I was hoping for some statement about imminent fortune without any need for fame. I wanted her to see me in a big house, with movie deals and best-selling novels. Not this.

"He's saying: *Tell him I'm sorry. Tell him I did my best. I'm sorry son, I did my best...*"

A disco ball was throwing lights around the ceiling, creating artificial stars. Someone was rubbing tones out of a Tibetan Singing Bowl. A girl on the next table was having a drawing done of her Spirit Guide, while a young man near the stage was getting a shiatsu massage and looking very uncomfortable. I felt very small, a little boy again. I couldn't find my voice at all.

"Is there nothing you want to ask?" said the sybil surprised at my silence, taking it for disbelief, wanting a chance to prove her seership with the £4.80 left on the clock. But I didn't need any more proof than that one sad phrase. It was my Dad, no doubt. I couldn't look her in the eye. I shook my head, and went to the car park behind the main street and cried.

I thought back to that crucial time when he first offered me the watch and opened it, unleashing momentarily all the agonies and failure of his own life and the fraught relationship with *his* Dad, his siblings, his wife and not least me – his only and rather snotty son.

I realised that it was not just a watch: it was a talisman and a time machine, a broken miniature of his dynasty's own mechanism. I knew that I'd have to have Dad's watch repaired, which was really *his* Dad's watch – and maybe the watch of everyone who has ever had a Dad and cried for them. And I'd have to find out what I could about this *G.M. Richardson, MM & Bar*, and why he went to War, and what he did that was so brave, and indeed what the 'War to end all Wars' was about in the first place, and why it never did.

Yes, I'd have to get that watch fixed and get the whole of my guilt-ridden internal workings, and the whole of my Dad's scattered family, put back together and ticking again...

2

INTO NO MAN'S LAND

Every time I think of Dad's Watch I get an image of an officer in the trenches of the Western Front looking at something very similar, trying very hard to keep himself from shaking, dreading the moment when the minute hand reached a certain number, and wondering if his world was about to end. He is blond, and has a long, narrow whistle in his very dry mouth. His thin moustache is beaded with sweat, his officer's uniform has been neatly pressed by his Soldier Servant; the buttons are polished and the braid just-so. *Tick tock tick tick...* and the cannons finish their softening up. He takes a deep breath and blows.

When I was a bolshy and thoroughly dreadful teenager that officer was always older and much bigger than me, an upper class twerp who knew exactly what he was involved in – and might even have deserved what was about to happen – capitalist running-dog that he was. When I get the same image now, in my sixth decade, having veered splendidly and sometimes manically from Maoist to Monarchist, I look at him staring down at the moving hands on the dial and think: *Poor young man. Run, run...*

So who was that young officer? Did I somehow 'remote view' an actual person? If we are deliberately creating an avatar of Geordie and his ilk, I think this young Rupert was a shoddy golem composed of my own youthful ignorance and prejudice, deliberately made to look handsome so that I could scorn him the more and sacrifice him accordingly.

It's a false memory, this image of the posh officer and the pocket watch; a flaky piece of clairvoyance. The officers were certainly upper class but they quickly learned to wear the uniform of privates, because the German snipers would spot the pips and buckles and braid from a mile away and shoot them to buggery. Plus they would have had *wrist* watches with a silver case, white dials and luminous hands, and although the Soldier Servant would have done his best, the uniform was inevitably still crawling with lice no matter how much he had burned the seams to try and destroy them. They might have been posh and privileged but they were also brave, fought their war as they understood it, and the dreadful casualty rate among young officers was proportionally much higher than that of their men.

But as someone who has always been subtly dominated by a whole range of quasi-autistic time anxieties, the officer looking at his pocket watch has been a compelling image for me over many years. As I started to research the war I had to readjust a lot of my prejudices about officers and men, battles and their effectiveness, parents and their children. I'm sure I got the shaking right, though.

In fact Grandad's timepiece never saw action unless it was in the smoky front room of his little home in Castle Terrace, Ashington, in the years after the Great War when he had to deal with his powerful wife and many small children.

I started writing all this during a long period of convalescence, after having bits cut out of my colon. This is a sure-fire surgical procedure designed to remind a man of the moving hands ticking his own life away, and rack his time-anxieties up a further notch. I was woken in the night by a semi-dream of that young officer but I knew deep down it wasn't right, and that my Dad and his Dad deserved more than an easy fantasy. So I started a frantic search for that folded paper napkin with the family details on it, because this was the accurate information that I needed. And there it was, glimpsed by torchlight at the top of a cupboard, still folded into a triangle and being used as a marker in a glossy little book about Ashington.[1]

I sat down in front of the dressing-table and saw myself in the mirror, a slightly gaunter version of the man I had been only two weeks before. Behind me, in the glooming, clothes hung in the open wardrobe like a platoon of assembled souls waiting for me to give them orders. I remembered a time 50 years before when I had looked at myself shivering in the mirror, in the middle of the night, in the bedroom in Ashington. The war between my parents seemed apocalyptic. The house was filled with screaming coils of barbed wire that would trap me and my sister however we tried to move, so that in the end we didn't, and just hung there absorbing shrapnel while praying for some Great Power to call a truce.

By every account, making what sense I could of the explosions of invective, my dad and mam were repeating exactly the same

---

1 *Hirst* by Mike Kirkup

patterns as had been enacted by those paternal grandparents I had never met. It was Mam who had all the artillery and a seemingly endless supply of shells. Even now, Pat and I can't fully understand why she was so hateful and we're still finding shrapnel fragments within ourselves. But as the years and the battles went on and on, it was apparent to me that I was failing to relate to my dad through the same behaviours and attitudes that he had used toward his own father. Despite this knowledge I couldn't find a way to end the war, and my powerful Mam egged me on anyway.

And all this family rage and torment seemed, in retrospect, to date back to the time when Grandad had fought his battles in Flanders and probably brought them all back home to Ashington along with his medals and scars, both mental and physical.

If I'd known anything of the Ancient Greek doomed-family myths I might have sought some comfort in those. As it was I looked at myself in the mirror, a skinny boy in striped pyjamas, and said: *It stops with me*. Though I couldn't have explained how I could stop it, or even what *it* was.

So there I was in 2012, far from the battlefields of my childhood and a grandfather myself, looking through my own reflection toward that little boy to whom I owed a debt. Before me was the old napkin on which my much-scattered family was preserved. I smoothed it out carefully, pressed it flat. Got a nice thick piece of parchment, and transferred all the names onto it with the respect I should have shown years before. Here were my paternal grandparents plus all my aunts, uncles and scattered cousins on that side of the family. Those aunts and uncles had all passed away. My sister still lived up in Ashington. My cousins, whom I only ever met once at my niece's wedding 25 years before, were scattered across London, Devon, Yorkshire and Spain, plus a long-lost cousin somewhere in America.

With these few details, and the dedication on the back of the watch itself to *Private G.M. Richardson*, I decided to reconstruct an era, and a family, and make sense of what that tough old bugger went through.

I looked at myself one more time in the mirror.
It starts with me I said...

It was never going to be possible to do a straightforward, sequential narrative about Geordie's war. Too much of his personal history had been blown to smithereens, the bits and pieces arcing over a vast area and most of them rotting away to nothingness in the quagmire of family indifference. The staff at the National Archives attempted to see what they could find from the few details I had sent them, but warned that 60% of the personnel records for the First World War had been destroyed or damaged during the Blitz of the Second World War.

Them bliddy Jarmins again! did I hear Dad say?

By this time I had stopped worrying whether it really was my Dad's spirit communicating with me, or was simply a guilt-driven literary device whereby I could have the banter with him after death that I could, should and dearly wanted to have during his lifetime, but never managed. Some things you've just got to get on with.

So while I was waiting for the results of their searches, and those by the volunteers at the Royal Northumberland Fusiliers Museum at Alnwick, I started to create what I suppose would now be called an avatar of him, using the fragments I had, fitting them all together, filling in the gaps with simple research and perhaps some dodgy intuition to make him come alive. I thought I would try to recreate him, not simply in my image, but as an image of a whole Northumbrian tribe as it got made lousy and blasted by the Great War. Although he was a very real and specific individual, in a sense I wanted to see him as Everyman and understand the First World War through his eyes.

I even had a photograph to inspire me, of him in his uniform. I don't remember where I got this. In contrast to many of the photographs taken of new recruits at this time, when some of the young men already have a look of doom about them, Grandad looks fit, cheerful, dark haired and handsome, proud of his uniform and ready for anything.

George Matthew Richardson M.M. & Bar was thus the name of my grandad, and also the essence of his kind. *Geordie's War* might more exactly be called *Geordies' War,* in the sense he wasn't just any Geordie, he was an über-Geordie.

Eh? said my Dad in my right brain again, because he never liked it when I got pompous and tried to use language to impress.

Oh Dad man, it means... the ultimate, above all, the best, top, something that nothing is better than. Aye, it's Jarmin.

But how can I justify Grandad as this super-Geordie, other than through family pride? Quite easily bonny lads. He:

* was born and raised in Scotswood Road
* worked as a machinist in Armstrong's factory
  (both of these being crucial to the Geordie anthem known as 'The Blaydon Races')
* spent some time as a miner
* loved his football
* liked his beer and became a barman in the Grand Hotel in Ashington, where three roads met at the very centre of the town which always prided itself as 'the biggest mining village in the world'
* adored his children but was probably frightened of his wife
* showed in a very quiet way, on the battlefield, that he was hard as fuck.

I'll come back to all of these later.

My Dad and Grandad bore the same name: George Matthew Richardson.

As we'll see, anyone in Northumberland with the name George was invariably called Geordie – which is a name that has come to describe the whole Northumbrian peoples. Grandad was therefore Big Geordie, and until he came to tower over everyone with a physique like Johnny Weismuller, Dad was Little Geordie.

Grandad was born in 1882; Dad in 1913. I have to use these dates as kind of temporal bookmarks, so I can quickly remind myself where one age sludges into the next, and realise where I'm standing. I do the same with my own life, marking the stages according to my children's births, and what I was doing when. In the Richardson Dynasty, if I may call it that, it seems to have been a marked tradition that sons were given exactly the same name as their fathers, but without with the suffixes Snr. or Jr. as would be the case in America.

Maybe it was to do with the high rates of mortality in pre-War generations, so the males would have a fighting chance of their names enduring. Northumberland in 1911 saw the highest infant

Private George Matthew Richardson M.M. & Bar

mortality rates in England, at 136 deaths per thousand live births. Almost twice as many as for rural Wiltshire where I now live, and considerably higher than London. Rural Northumberland was (and still is) more like Dartmoor than anywhere else, and as sparsely populated; most of the deaths would have been concentrated in the heavily industrialised areas along the Tyne, in Newcastle itself, and in that dark satanic stretch of coal fields which extended up toward Ashington, some 20 miles north.

Ironically, by the very end of the War in 1918 the infant mortality rate in that area had actually fallen to 103 deaths per thousand, and this was quite likely to have been because the food rationing introduced in February of that year gave them a better diet than many of them had had before.

Reading the on-line Census details for my family from 1841 onward, it is clear that when a child died the name was often retained and given to a later issue. So that when little May Richardson died around the year 1917 (and Dad always said it was due to 'starvayshun') we see something of her spirit restored when a later girl was called Doris May.

In the eyes of the two Geordies, boys were important because – in those days – only they could get proper work. If you didn't work then quite simply you died of hunger because there was no system of Benefits then, or National Health Service. And boys kept the family name too and if your name survives then your spirit carries on. Tribal peoples since time began could tell you that much. Although my Dad adored his grandchildren they were all girls; hence his fear that one of them might marry someone 'stupid' who would get his watch and sell it. I'm not sure that he entirely trusted me in that respect either.

Or perhaps there was some inner trickster spirit which just wanted to cause confusion, so that the children of the male line never knew where one Dad ended and ourselves began. I think all men get something of that bewilderment when we shave in the mirror before going off to our own daily conflicts. We look at our reflections and the daft things we've done over the decades, and the strange little quirks we've developed and the hair coming out of our noses and ears, and cry out with either pride or horror: *I'm becoming my Dad…!*

The names George and William occur again and again down the centuries, and very close together. I myself would have been called George if my Dad had had his way. *No!* said The Mam – or more precisely *Ner!* She didn't want anyone else being called Little Geordie. So then he plumped for William, after his favourite brother who was a tough soldier in the Coldstream Guards. But The Mam sent up a rolling explosive barrage about that too and so he kept quiet.

Still, not unreasonably I suppose, she did argue that the initials W.A.R. would have made me look pretty stupid and attract a lot of flak when I started school. I've always felt there was something about my name which jarred, or was missing, and which floated about like a phantom limb making me twitchy, but I suppose I can accept this now.

This 'naming of the parts' as a poet of later war might have termed it, is not entirely self-indulgence. Thanks to these idiosyncrasies, and with the help of the long-dead General Haig, I was later able to track down those long lost medals of grandad's which some of his grandchildren didn't even know existed in the first place.

They were in South Carolina – where else?

As I sent out requests for information, wrote endless letters, logged onto websites that seemed to go dead even as I scrolled down them, made phone calls to bemused cousins I scarcely knew and who knew less about our grandparents than I did, and just dipped into library books at random in order to learn something about the Great War, there was one single date which kept cropping up hammering at my mind quite as much as 1882 and 1913:

July 1st 1916. This was the first day of one particular battle.

Make a temporal bookmark of this yourselves, because whether you know it or not the events of this day are still buried deep and will rise beneath your skin at unexpected times like shrapnel, so you'll try to cut the bits out. At that time I still didn't know if Geordie had actually fought there, but I knew I needed to look briefly just at the events on this one date in order to get some sense of what was pure insanity.

This was the first day of The Somme.

On that date, at 7.30 in the morning, the British and Commonwealth Armies were stretched silently along almost 20 miles of both banks of the River Somme, which flowed through Picardy in northern France. The name Somme comes from a Celtic word meaning 'tranquillity', and there are distinctly ironic echoes of it in words like somnolent, or somnambulist, or even somatic.

It was a pretty enough place in essence. The great French novelist Victor Hugo was inspired to write: 'There's nothing prettier than the banks of the Somme... the water flowing beautifully between the reeds, the exquisite islands of the river in their midst.'[2]

Philéas Lebesgue, a native of the area and a symbolist poet who was constantly inspired by nature and rural life almost sang when as a young man he penned the lines: 'Oh! The Earth is truly made of flesh, a living flesh.'[3]

Picardy was calm, beautiful and bucolic.

Eh? Bucolic: is that a drink problem?
Dad it means rustic, pastoral, suggesting an idyllic rural life.

Even so, Picardy has had long martial associations with our past. The invasion fleet of William the Conqueror (more accurately called William the Bastard) had once assembled at Saint-Valery-sur-Somme, in that crucial year of 1066. If the English under Harold Godwinson hadn't been exhausted after their long march down from Stamford Bridge, after defeating a Viking army, and if the Normans hadn't had stirrups so they could fight from horseback, they'd never have won, not ever, and women probably would have had full equality by the 13th Century.

The River Somme also featured in 1346 when Edward III's army forded at the battle of Blanchetaque, during the campaign which led to the Battle of Crécy. And also in the campaign which ended at Agincourt, when we showed them what could be done with longbows, hammers, axes and the common man's total disregard for the rules of chivalry.[4]

---

2 Victor Hugo 1802-1885. Best known here for *Les Miserables*, and *The Hunchback of Notre Dame*
3 1869-1958
4 The heavily-armoured French knights, when dislodged from their horses by the longbows, lay in the mud expecting that they would be helped up, given adequate respect and lodgings, and kept for ransom. That's how wars were fought then: only the commoners got slaughtered; that's what commoners

A number of the well-educated officers lined up that day would have been well aware of these historical associations. In the minds of a few there would be pennons flying and glories to be reaped: *mater* and *pater* and the headmasters of their old schools would be ever so proud. Second Lieutenant Siegfried Sassoon recalled that the weather that morning was simply heavenly. There were 158,000 British soldiers of all ranks in place, superbly trained, filled with spirit and the highest ideals – and they were all volunteers, not a conscript among them. In a few minutes after the whistles blew, the lucky ones would find themselves clinging onto the ground by their eyelids.

The British Generals responsible for all this – Haig and Rawlinson – prepared to watch the preliminary artillery barrage from the heights of Querrieu, 12 miles behind the front lines. The whole strategy was called by them The Big Push. It's almost a jolly term, suggestive of the manly, character-building japes you might find at the Eton Wall Game, and they were determined that none of the British divisions would ever show themselves to be 'windy' or 'sticky' when it came to pushing. Haig, an old cavalryman, had some doubts about the New Army battalions with ridiculous names like the Artists Rifles, Barnsley Pals, Newcastle Commercials, Glasgow Boys Brigade Pals, Newcastle Railway Pals – and far worse. A carefully drafted Special Order had been read out to some of these, which included the warning: 'The use of the word retire is absolutely forbidden, and if heard can only be a ruse of the enemy and must be ignored.'

The generals themselves had been compelled by their French allies to launch this attack earlier than planned in the hope of relieving the enormous pressure much further along the front at Verdun, where the Germans seemed to be in imminent danger of breaking through. If that ever happened and they got to the coast and controlled the all-important ports then civilisation as we knew it would end.

The plan was simple. After a huge artillery barrage lasting one week and firing 1,800,000 shells which would completely subdue the opposition, they would smash through the enemy lines and create a gap which Haig's beloved cavalry would exploit, with sabres flashing, the horses leaping across the triple rows of defensive

---

were for. The English and Welsh footsoldiers broke all the rules of Continental chivalry by setting about the floundering chevaliers with hammers and knives, using their halberds like tin-openers.

trenches and clearing the way for a total rout and the end of the war. It would all be over by tea-time, chaps!

It was a total disaster.

Despite the intensity of a barrage which could be heard from Hampstead Heath in North London, the German soldiers were largely untouched in their deep and reinforced shelters. The British attackers were so burdened down by the weight of their equipment – each Tommy carried upward of 70 lbs – they could scarcely walk, never mind make swift attacking movements, though none of them could ever have been called 'sticky' in their actions that morning. None of them, capitalist or communist, atheist or High Church, deserved what they went through. The German machine-gunners climbed out of their deep holes, set themselves up on the edge of the craters and had plenty of time to pick their targets.

The Battle of the Somme, as it became known, started on the 1st July and rumbles in the British psyche yet. By the end of that one day the British had suffered 19,240 dead, 35,493 wounded, 2,152 missing and 585 prisoners for a total loss of 57,470. A few researchers have argued for even higher figures than that, but none for any less.

One day. To achieve what?

Sweet bugger all. Sweet Fanny Adams! said Dad, swearing in my head like I never heard him swear out loud. One hundred years after that first day of The Somme say those phrases again and again and never forget them. We achieved sweet bugger all and were never likely to.

There were so many corpses that when people later came to dig into the soil of the Somme the shovels didn't strike earth, they struck meat. It was as if the entire population of, say, Geordie's town of Ashington went out for breakfast and just disappeared, never to be heard from again; with all the adjoining towns of Amble, Bedlington, Morpeth, Newbiggin and Blyth receiving a least one seriously wounded person per household.

Or to help you grasp the ungraspable nature of this in another way, imagine that every word in this book, and all its punctuation, represented a body. And that was just the first day.

General Haig wrote in his diary on July 2nd: "...the total casualties are estimated at over 40,000 to date. This cannot be considered severe in view of the numbers engaged, and the length of front attacked."[5] He wanted to start it all over again, and give it another go, a Bigger Push, and when he died in 1928 he was still arguing that cavalry would have an important role to play in every future war.

By the so-called 'end' of that one battle in late November that year, the British and French casualties of killed, wounded or missing came to 623,907. Compare that to the 450,900 total civilian and military casualties suffered by the British during the six years of World War 2, and you might get more of an idea.

General Haig and his Big Push. What a plan that was. Or so it seemed to me at first.

I'll come back to him later, if only to express bewilderment at the knowledge that vast numbers of old soldiers of all ranks paid respects at his state funeral in 1928, and that Grandad had enormous admiration for the man. War, like family relationships, can throw up some bewildering contradictions when looked at from the outside, creating puzzles that might never be explained or even be explicable, and often leaving a lot of high explosives just below the surface.

After taking a peek at just this one day of July 1st, of just this one battle which actually thundered on for several months, I realised that it was not simply that I wanted to learn how Geordie fitted into the War to end all Wars as H.G. Wells termed it. No, it became more a case of seeing the Why to start all Whys, and the urge to understand how, on the following day of July 2nd 1916, ordinary folk like Big Geordie Richison, as they would have pronounced it, did not start a revolution...

---

5   Robertshaw, Andrew (2006). *Somme 1 July 1916: Tragedy and Triumph.* Osprey Publishing. p. 70.

3

OVER THE TOP AND FAR BELOW

NORTHUMBERLAND provided 51 battalions during the Great War – second only to the London Regiment. The War Memorial in Ashington today bears three plaques inscribed with a total of 746 names and dedicated to: 'The Glory of God and the Glorious Memory of those Inhabitants of Ashington and District who gave their lives for their country in the Great War 1914–1918.' The vast majority of them are shown as having served in the NF, or Northumberland Fusiliers.

There is a fourth plaque dedicated to the victims of World War II, and this bears 151 names. Only 11 of them served with what by then had become the Royal Northumberland Fusiliers; most of them seem to have opted for the RAF.

Anything, perhaps, to avoid becoming Poor Bloody Infantry and having their faces shoved in the clarts again.

As a bairn I never really noticed the War Memorial. Those plaques were originally installed outside a ward of Ashington Hospital. After World War II, when the ward was demolished, they were moved to Ashington Cricket Clubhouse. Eventually, after a long campaign by ex-servicemen in the town to give the dead of two world wars a fitting monument, Wansbeck Council organised a competition to find the best design. They settled on a cubic structure that was heavily pebble-dashed, and surmounted by the sort of avant-garde, cheap-and-nasty art that seemed more appropriate for getting reception on the new 625-line tellies that were all the rage then.

I'd like to have been there and heard the comments when they unveiled it.

Ah waz there, said Dad. *Hey mind, it was like a bunch o' bliddy coat-hangers.*[6]

---

6 The coat-hangers have now been replaced with a dignified statue of a soldier.

The point is, this rather pitiful structure aimed at honouring nearly 1000 individuals killed in two World Wars was dwarfed by the memorial erected to the 13 men killed by a gas explosion in the Woodhorn Colliery Disaster of 13th August 1916. Which occurred just weeks after the opening day of the Somme Offensive.

As the Ashington miners were dying far underground, after having tried to drive a drift from the Low Main to the High Main, their marras[7] in the Fusiliers were involved in vicious combat at the battles of Flers-Courcelette, including the infamous High Wood. Ironically it was probably Northumbrian ex-miners who helped dig tunnels under the German lines in order to lay explosives below the machine-gun posts.

Every person in Ashington and District today is familiar with that tall and sombre obelisk surmounted by the statue of the pitman with his pick-axe and lamp and knows that it commemorated something sad. While not trying to diminish the horror of this mining disaster by invidious comparison, not

---

[7] Friends

one in ten thousand will know anything about the agonies that their lads went through at High Wood.[8]

On the surface of it, the folk of Ashington seem to have had a more deeply ingrained allegiance to King Coal than King George. Then again, as we will see, they probably weren't being told everything about what was going on in France and Flanders.

Although I'm told they've moved the statue of the coal miner now, it towered for years in the Floor Park,[9] where Dad used to take me on Sunday mornings to watch the old gadgies in their flat caps playing bowls. (I think I was about 16 before I met anyone in Ashington who went to church. The small Catholic community was more devout: if you went to Mass, you were allowed to go to Bingo afterward.)

I liked the Floor Park, and the wooden shelters and the flat lawns of the bowling greens and the fresh air. Sure, the water fountain was jammed with gravel and the large pond was toxic olive green and probably evolving the sort of life forms that would one day cause havoc in the nightclubs of the Bigg Market in Newcastle, but everything in the park was clean and still. Don't get me wrong, I loved Ashington as a lad, and still do, but the streets were later to be described on television as 'quagmires of dog obscenity' and that wasn't far wrong. Use Google Earth to view the former colliery rows even today and you won't see many trees in the area known as the Hirst. And don't zoom too close because they still love their dogs up there.

This particular morning we'd escaped from another of The Mam's onslaughts, and left my older sister Pat to mop up after the thrown plates and the emotional carnage.

"What's wrang wi' Mam?" I asked, running along the slats of the benches, with their flaking green paint and rusting iron supports, with my cowboy hat fastened firmly under my chin and imagining

---

8   It has been estimated that the ground there still contains the remains of some 8,000 British and German soldiers who were killed in action. Even today, parts of the wood conceal live ammunition and it is unsafe to stray from the paths.
9   Flower Park

I was Hopalong Cassidy. I was about four, and grossly immature compared to the other kids, who were already playing tiggy with hatchets.

The sun was glinting off the head of the stone miner, whose helmet and shoulders were always white with droppings, like an early form of high-visibility jacket. Dad pushed his own cloth cap back and lolled his head against the shelter and closed his eyes to try and blot out things.

"Dr McPhorson said it wuz The Change," he said softly, to himself, as if it might explain things, though it never would. He knew I wouldn't understand and I didn't. He would never have guessed I would remember, but I do.

Two men he knew walked past and nodded to him. They'd had a bit of trouble 10 years ago at some place called Arnhem, he told me almost wistfully.

I drew my silver six-gun and loaded it with a roll of caps, leaped to the end of the shelter so the sun was behind me and took a careful aim.

"What did *you* do in the war Dad?" I asked, to distract him as I lined up the shot.

He frowned. That was clearly a sore point. I realise now that everyone would have known about his own Dad the War Hero, M.M. & Bar and all that, and also about his brother Bill who had fought bravely in Tobruk for the elite Coldstream Guards.

"Ah was a Bevin Boy, me," he said.

He told me this with a small drop of pride that was quickly dissolved in a huge bowl of exasperation. It meant nothing, but I remembered that name too.

"Put ya hands up!" I shouted, taking a firm stance, sparrow-legs apart.

He did, and I pulled the trigger and the cap went CRACK! and I got him, right between the eyes.

When the First World War was declared there was a wave of collective insanity which caused young men to volunteer in vast numbers.

It is easy but not necessarily accurate to use that term 'insanity' in the 21st century however. In 1914 it was a matter of enthusiasm and loyalty to the country. They knew what they were doing even if they didn't know exactly what they were going into. Then again, no-one did.

Recruiting numbers were so large that the Home Front started suffering: the skilled operatives were no longer there to operate all those machineries which were needed for the country to work. When the situation became dire they brought women into the factories, but they were never sent down the mines. In certain areas the coalition government had to introduce a reverse form of conscription to bring vital workers back from the military.

By the time the Second World War was declared the government had learned the lessons of the earlier conflict, and Ernest Bevin told the coal miners of Britain:

"We need 720,000 men continuously employed in this industry. This is where you boys come in. Our fighting men will not be able to achieve their purpose unless we get an adequate supply of coal."

I already knew that much. Apparently Dad had tried to join up in 1939 and 'do his bit' but was turned away. What I didn't know was that a number of conscientious objectors were sent to work down the mines as an alternative to military service.

Were you a conchie, Dad?
Ner son, Ah didn't have the nerve. Brave lads, them conchies.

When the recruiting started during the Great War the men of Ashington had a choice: glorious military service for a wee while with their marras in the legendary and elite Northumberland Fusiliers; or a continuous lifetime doon the Pits – and there were plenty of those.

Though if you really were a Conchie and got sent down the pit to punish you for your beliefs, you'd also get the sort of treatment that would make you wish you were in Flanders after all. Many men who remained on the Home Front doing vital work argued that they should have been provided with uniforms also, to avoid the constant invective from those who saw them as shirkers.

Even in late 1918, when stories of what the war was *really* like had filtered back home, Ashington was still able to raise the 4th (Volunteer) Battalion Northumberland Fusiliers. There is a photograph of them posing in front of what looks suspiciously like the old Portland Hotel before they modernised and expanded it.[10] There are 58 men in uniform and three earnest-looking civilians flanking them. A few of them look far too old to be going to war; a couple look as if they should still be at school. Although it was termed a 'volunteer' battalion there really wasn't an option at this point. Enlist and you could join a regiment already filled with men familiar to you; wait to get conscripted and you could be sent anywhere.

I suppose if you have to get the avatar of Big Geordie Richardson energised and running, you've now got to have some insight into the very nature of Geordieness.

So why were the Northumbrians called Geordies in the first place?

The clue is in the lamp held by the statue of that miner in the Floor Park. The story goes that George Stephenson of Killingworth Colliery invented a lamp in 1815 which gave far greater brightness than any other device. It also used a system whereby if there was a high level of firedamp in the atmosphere underground, it would extinguish itself and thereby prevent an explosion.

Most of the other miners in other parts of the country used lamps invented by Humphry Davy from Cornwall, which tended to become too hot, and – according to the northern critics – never gave the same level of illumination.

So it was down to miner rivalry that all those workers north of the Tyne became known as Geordies, rather than Humphrys, which is a good thing if you ask me. I've never heard a miner argue any different.

Not all historians agree with this. They argue that the name was derived from the Jacobite Rebellion of 1745 when the people of Newcastle were seen as staunch

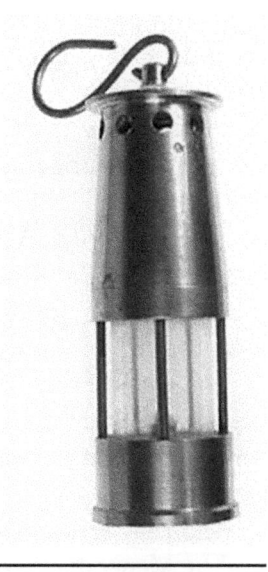

---

10 Its landlord once opined to me, with weariness: *The young lads there would rather fight than fuck.*

supporters of the Hanoverian King George II, and were thus 'Geordie Whelps', a punning play on the term 'George the Guelph'. Hence the story about the lamps is something of a *canard* in their eyes. Though as my Dad might have commented: *What would a French duck knaa aboot being a Geordie eh?*

Why do they flutter their Geordieness into the conversation at every opportunity, and love it when you can't understand? And why would Big Geordie feel that being a Geordie was so important that he would want to leave his wife and children and join up and fight for the Northumberland Fusiliers?

I think there might a tribal thing involved in this. Two thousand years ago the occupying Romans would have called them the Votadini, and they seem to have had a lot of trouble with them. The Legions had rolled over the Durotriges, Dobunni and Cornovii, crushed the Iceni and Catuvellauni and all the rest (apart from a few sleepless nights caused by that canny lass Boadicea, whom I've heard argued was a typical Geordie woman). They were stopped short by the Votadini.

Even today the children of Northumberland are told by their tongue-in-cheek dads that Hadrian's Wall had really been built to keep the Geordies oot, because Rome was so scared of them. You can picture it:

Veni, Vidi, Vici! cried the massed Legions on the southern side of the Wall, bashing their shields with their little swords and chewing their garlic.

HADDAWAY AN' SHITE came the answer from the proto-Fusiliers on the Geordie side before they strolled off with their tattooed lasses to make strong sons in the Wild Hills of the Wannies.

You can see the same strands of DNA in action today when the Newcastle United supporters travel to the Soft Sooth and stand bare-chested on the terraces of opposing teams in February, to show how hard they are.

And they are.

The Venerable Bede, writing at the end of the 7th Century in his monastery at Jarrow, described anyone north of the Tyne as Irish, for reasons that we needn't go into now. (It was interesting that when Big Jack Charlton from Ashington became manager of the Irish football team he announced that he felt Irish, aye, he really did! And I know exactly what he meant.) It has also been said that the Old English heroic epic poem *Beowulf* translates more successfully into Geordie than into modern-day English.

Ah canna see that, son. And nor could I.

Curiously, the actual name George is derived from the Greek word *georgos* meaning farmer, or earthworker, as it derives from the elements (*ge*) 'earth' and (*ergon*) 'work'. And one of the symbols for the Royal Northumberland Fusiliers of later years was that of St George on horseback slaying the dragon.

Get on with it Alan.

Look bonny lads it's simple: the Geordies regarded themselves as the Lords of the Working Classes, and when it came to the war, them Jarmins were nivver ganna knaa what hit them.[11]

---

11 I was present at a research project lasting one long liquid evening in the Hirst East End & District, CIU Affiliated, Working Man's Social Club, when it was effectively proven and agreed by all concerned that one Northumberland Fusilier was equal tae five Jarmins, ten Japs, or a thoosand Eyeties.

4

ASHINGTON, AND OTHER BATTLEFIELDS

OTHER people's genealogies are invariably tedious, so I'll be quick with mine, and get to those necessary details that will help us understand our man. Thus:

George Matthew Richardson married Jane Isabella Yellowley on the 24th of February 1912. He gave his 'Rank or Profession' as Barman, and his address as 81 Castle Terrace, Hirst, Ashington. His age was noted as being 27 and his 'Condition' as Bachelor. Jane was a 24-year-old Spinster who was then living at 13 Chestnut Street, Ashington.

Both fathers attended. Thomas Richardson was noted as a Cranesman, from Armstrong's Factory in Newcastle, and John Yellowley was a Coal-miner (Hewer) – as was added in brackets. That could have been at any one of a dozen mines in the Ashington area. He would have insisted on adding the term 'Hewer' because that showed he was the hardest of the hard, working at the very bottom of the pit, at the end of the tunnel, howking away at the coal seams with his pick by the light of his Geordie lamp. I imagine that he might have felt that Thomas Richardson, as a mere Cranesman, was a bit of a softie. He certainly had no respect for his shitey son.

After the wedding at the local Registry Office in nearby Morpeth, the happy couple went to live at Castle Terrace where they produced the first three of their seven children.

The simple details on the wedding certificate were like dog-tags: producing a huge surge of information when put in context. Especially when collated with the stuff I'd already tracked down online via the ten-yearly Census records.

First, Geordie was working as a barman at the Grand Hotel in Ashington, which is where he met Jane, whose profession was given elsewhere as 'Servant'.

Second, his father's name enabled me to pinpoint exactly where in Newcastle, among all the other unrelated Richardsons, his family originally came from.

Third, the little bugger had lied about his age because he was 30 when he married, not 27.

And fourth, the happy couple was probably a very worried couple, and their Dads were almost certainly puffing on their Wild Woodbine tabs[12] with annoyance, because at the time of their marriage Jane was nearly 3 months pregnant.

Looking through the Census records was always a fascinating and often moving experience, knowing that these complete strangers had helped create me. I had no desire to fashion the usual Family Tree with all its hanging branches: my brain can't process that sort of information. I just grabbed onto Thomas and his known son George and followed a straight line back from 1911, 1901, 1891 and so on until 1841, whizzing back like Rod Taylor in the *The Time Machine* and wondering what Morlocks I might find along the way.

Those details aren't relevant here but it made me chuckle when I could almost see the assorted gentlemen from the Census Bureau

---

12 cigarettes

trying to grasp the accent, often giving up and putting down the nearest equivalent. Thus Maypole Street in Ashington caused me some bewilderment until I said it *à la* Geordie, flattening and almost gutturalising the 'a' and contracting the final syllable until I got it... Maple Street. Maybe the *Beowulf* theory was right after all.

Browsing those ancient Census sheets, using the right click of the mouse to zoom in and slowly decipher the handwriting was like looking through the pages of the Necronomicon, which –

Eh?

Necronomicon, Dad. It means 'Book of Dead Names'.

Whey could ye not just say that? Not ivvrybody went tae Ashin'ton bliddy Grammar School ye knaa![13]

Point taken.

What really enabled the burgeoning avatar to grow wings (or at least put on uniform) was the arrival of two files from the National Archives showing that at least some of Grandad's documents had escaped the Blitz, proving that he had survived everything the Germans had thrown at him. In the event, these threw up more mysteries than they solved.

Even now I don't know the proper name for these little cards, which must have fitted quite nicely into some index system in London. I'll call them Medal Cards because one of them jumped right out at me as being labelled:

Awarded the Military Medal. Richardson, G.M. Regimental Number 4214. 6th Bn North'd Fus. TF.

There were actually 11 other similar cards on the pdf documents giving details of other Richardsons from the Great War. There were even two others which bore the name Richardson, George M. I assumed this was just the commonality of the name, as the regimental numbers didn't match. The second gave Richardson G.M. as being a private in the Northumberland Fusiliers but with the number 37829. The third, I was eventually able to discount.

It took me a few weeks to make sense of all this, and find out how the same man could have two regimental numbers and belong to both the 6th and 13th Battalion of the same regiment.

---

13 As the dad of four very different girls, each brilliant in their own ways, I am totally against Grammar Schools.

It would be quite possible if, after having served in the front line and won his M.M. and Bar[14] and also being nominated for the D.C.M. (as I later learned), he had 'copped a Blighty One'. That is, a wound which was enough to get you sent home and hopefully not enough to cripple you for life. Then, honourably discharged and back home in Ashington, the daft sod went and re-enlisted to serve back at the Front as a non-combatant stretcher bearer in the same regiment.

I sit here taking in that scenario and my jaw drops. I shake my head in wonder.

Ah nivver knew that either, son, said Dad who was born in 1913.
Balls of Steel, I think.
Steel's not hard enough. Diamond, Ah reckon.
Balls of Diamond then.
And ye knaa what diamonds are made of?
Coal...

⁂

We've got enough material now to send Geordie gannin' alang to St George's Drill Hall in Newcastle, get him enlisted and then fitted up in his Fusiliers uniform. Although our avatar would look mighty smart, he'd still be something of a hollow man at this stage. Something else is needed.

On the same day as I got these details from the National Archives I got news from Tupra, the watch and clock repairers in Abbey Green, Bath, just opposite that Emporium where Dad had first offered me Grandad's watch. The watch could be fixed, though it would take a couple of months.

Champion! said Dad.

I thought it was appropriate to leave it with them, not least because the man behind the counter declared it to be an exceptional watch, very unusual, but because I felt he had the sort of honest face that would never dream of removing the jewels. I still photographed it externally and internally, close-up and at every angle with an 18 mega-pixel camera before I let him have it though.

Apart from the relatively cosmetic stuff of replacing the glass and fixing the dial it needed a new main spring – which Dad had

---

14 'and Bar' means it was awarded again.

told me years ago. In these days of quartz movements youngsters are unaware of how the old devices worked, needing winding at least once a day, and always the danger of over-winding, so that the main spring stuck and wouldn't uncoil. I think we all know how that feels.

Y'see all mechanical watches have five parts: a mainspring, gear train, balance wheel, escapement mechanism and dial. The main spring is made of a long strip of hardened and blued steel coiled around the spindle known as the *arbor*, with the inner end hooked to that. The spring is wound up by turning the arbor one way, and then the force as it uncoils turns the arbor the other way, to run the clock by a series of beautifully meshing gears.

And the jewels? They were used as bearings because their low friction improved the watch accuracy as well as prolonging its bearing life. Manufacturers listed the number of jewels prominently on the watch face or back, as an advertising point. A typical fully jewelled pocket watch like Dad's had 17 jewels: two cap jewels, two pivot jewels, an impulse jewel for the balance wheel, two pivot jewels, two pallet jewels for the pallet fork, and two pivot jewels each for the escape, fourth, third, and centre wheels.

Of course I don't understand that for one moment and it has all been lifted from *Wikipedia* anyway, but I had to shut Dad up didn't I?

The poetic imagery here was immediate and immense. But who was the mainspring in all this lot, and who – or what – was the arbor?

Doing my Hopalong Cassidy quick-draw and shooting from the hip, I'm pretty certain that the mainspring was, of course, Grandad himself. There he was, a piece of hardened steel, beaten and bent by forces higher than greater than himself into the coiled shape necessary for the machineries of his universe to work.

As to the arbor, I've a strong suspicion we might find that along the Scotswood Road...

Come on, you've all heard it. It has been thrumming below the surface of your mind all along. Here's the shortened version. Let rip...

Ah went ter Blaydon Races, 'twas on the ninth of Joon,
Eiteen hundred an' sixty-two, on a summer's efternoon;
Aw tyuk the bus frae Balmbra's, an' she wis heavy laden,
Away we went doon Collingwood Street, that's on the road ter Blaydon.

(chorus)

Oh! me lads, ye shud a' seen us gannin,
Passin' the folks alang the road just as they were stannin'.
Theres aall the lads and lasses there, aall wi' smiling faces
Gannin' alang the Scotswood Rooooaaaad ter see the Blaydon Races!

We flew past Airmstrang's factory, and up to the 'Robin Adair',
Just gannin' doon te the railway bridge, the bus wheel flew off there.
The lasses lost their crinolines, an' the veils that hide their faces,
Ah got two black eyes an' a broken nose in gan ter Blaydon Races…

There's more, but you get the drift. This is the Geordie Anthem. They know the words of this better than they know that ditty about God saving the Queen and Phil the Greek. The Blaydon Races still exist, for anyone interested, and you might want to google them for as happy a day as you're ever likely to have.[15] But it's Armstrong's factory and the Scotswood Road we need to look at now.

The adjoining districts of Scotswood, Elswick and Benwell grew up during the Industrial Revolution and provided the labour for the huge complex of Armstrong factories that eventually developed, plus the innumerable coal mines that gave rise to the old phrase about 'bringing coals to Newcastle' i.e. expending a lot of time and energy doing something utterly useless or redundant.

The genius behind this area was one William Armstrong who invented and developed the Hydraulic Crane in 1845, and it was this state-of-the-art piece of engineering which caused people to

---

15 http://www.blaydonrace.org

flock there for jobs and made Armstrong's fortune. The Scotswood Road area was not so much a Silicone Valley, but a valley of steel and coal, water, fire and air. Or a very clarty version of the Klondike.

He was an extraordinary man, Armstrong, and an early advocate of renewable energy, predicting as early as 1863 that England would cease to produce coal within two centuries. He got that just about right. As well as the use of hydroelectricity he also felt that solar power in tropical areas had a major future, as an acre of ground could receive enough energy from the sun that, if properly harnessed, would release the 'amazing power of 4000 horses' acting for nearly nine hours every day.

As to the use of his inventions for war, he didn't have too many qualms. He said once: "If I thought that war would be fomented, or the interests of humanity suffer, by what I have done, I would greatly regret it. I have no such apprehension... It is our province, as engineers, to make the forces of matter obedient to the will of man; those who use the means we supply must be responsible for their legitimate application."[16]

Slippery sod, eh? 'Divvin't blame me, blame the politicians' Ah knaa his sort.

Aye Dad, aye...

I had to say that because if he got started on Thatcher it would feel like the Field Punishment Number One they used to dish out in the Great War, when they'd lash you to a wagon wheel for hours at a time, sometimes in range of enemy fire.

The Armstrong Whitworth company merged with Vickers to become known as Vickers-Armstrong. It expanded into one of the most important warship manufacturers in the world, with shipyards at Elswick and Walker, an aircraft assembly plant at Gosforth, arms factories at Elswick, Scotswood and Birtley, plus a shell manufacturing shop at Darlington which was managed by the North Eastern Railway on their behalf. They later turned their martial genius into the creation of these new-fangled tanks, the designs of one being pinched by the Germans in the late 1920s and becoming the first of their Panzers. Later still, by the time of the

---

[16] Dougan, David (1970). *The Great Gun-Maker: The Story of Lord Armstrong.* Sandhill Press Ltd

Second World War, Supermarine Aviation Works (Vickers) Ltd was responsible for producing the legendary Spitfire.

Among the innovative engineers he attracted to his factory at Elswick in the early days were Andrew Noble and George Wightwick Rendel whose design of gun-mountings and hydraulic control of gun-turrets were adopted world-wide. Rendel also developed the cruiser as a naval vessel, creating a kind of greyhound of the seas when the situation needed something fast and nasty, with a real bite.

Here, in 1912, they helped craft the Vickers machine gun that was used so devastatingly only a couple of years later. And they churned out vast quantities of shells to be fired by their huge guns. More of those shells and guns later.

There were two particularly well-visited pubs in the area called *The Hydraulic Crane* and *The Gun*, which gives some idea of the area's tone. My Dad used to meet up with his uncles there until The Mam got him in her sights. I think she had some sort of psychic periscope which enabled her to anticipate and scan his movements. If the Vickers machine gun had a rate of fire of 450 rounds per minute, she could easily outdo this with the withering intensity and sheer genius of her invective, the very least of which was: *Yer aboot as much use as a nick in a coo's arse!* What could a man do but put his hands up and surrender?

So...

George Matthew Richardson – Big Geordie – was born on October 2nd 1882 and raised at 62 Rendel Street, Elswick, just off the Scotswood Road[17]. His dad at the time was a mere Cranesman. Being still at school in the 1891 Census, he was put down as a 'Scholar'.

By 1901, when they had moved along the road to 40 Rendel Street, Thomas Richardson was describing himself, rather proudly I would imagine, as an Hydraulic Craneman, so he must have been promoted. By then his son George was working as a machinist – presumably also in Armstrong's factory.

It's rather eerie to use the modern medium of *YouTube* and watch a clip of 20,000 workers pouring in to Lord Armstrong's Elswick Works, Newcastle, and realising that some of my long-

---

17 Rendel Street is no longer in existence; however, it is shown on the 1898 OS map as running south from Beaumont Street down onto Scotswood Road. It was a few streets eastwards of Elswick Colliery and west of the Cruddass Recreation Ground.

dead relatives might well be among the crowds – including Geordie himself. Note that all the workers wore cloth caps. And the bosses with top hats and bowlers keep wandering before the camera again and again.[18]

Scotswood Road, being central to all this, was the arbor I mentioned earlier around which the mainspring of the watch is coiled. That's where our Geordie was born, amid his working class community with its powerful sense of identity and shared values. That's where he got his Geordieness and it's where the power of the British Army sprang from, to set the whole world ticking before blasting it all to pieces.

By 1911 he was living as a boarder with Sam and Margaret Hart, at 3 Second Avenue, Ashington, while working as a barman at the Grand Hotel. There is a belief within the family that also he worked as a miner before this, though no-one knows any more detail than that.

The Grand, as everyone called it, was one of only three pubs in the town, the other two being the Portland Hotel and North Seaton Hotel – known universally as the White Elephant. It was demolished in the 1980s to make way for something totally uninteresting but the other two remain. Later, at the height of the coal mining boom, the small town also supported some 30 Working Men's Social Clubs, some of them quite magnificent inside. Coach tours would come from as far away as Glasgow for the period we all called 'Scotch Week' when they arrived en masse and attempted to show us all what *real* drinking wiz aall aboot. So the Geordies did and do like their beer.

When I took my wife into one of the surviving clubs only a few years ago the lasses behind the bar were charmingly but genuinely bewildered when she asked for a glass of wine. No-one had ever made that request before. Eventually, after raiding the cellars, they found something slightly fizzy left over from a wedding reception, and served it in a half-pint glass. We loved the place.

Although it was built in the 1890s the Grand Hotel never seemed to change.

---

18 http://www.youtube.com/watch?v=SwKKoUzJpq8

There is a photograph from 1934 of the inside, taken during one of Humphrey Spender's patronising forays on behalf of the Mass Observation social research organisation. Our Geordie was still working there then, and did so until he retired. When I first went there in the late 1960s it was eerily and uncannily the same.

Old men wearing cloth caps seated in a corner. Others hunched over the bar. No-one went out with their head uncovered. Two loose dogs which had peed on the stone floor, breaking all those Health and Safety rules which would make later generations apoplectic. And there was one gadgie, half-turned toward the camera, who drew my eye again and again. I felt sure it was Grandad.

Ah think that's him there Alan!
That's what I thought Dad but I have to be careful: I look for him everywhere, these days. He's in my head all the time.
Gaan canny son, gaan canny...

It always needs a certain stretch of the imagination to accept that the figures bearing all the wrinkles, twists and vestments of a greater age than yourself were once, also, horny little bastards who were up to every trick in the book and could teach us at least something about everything. Which brings us neatly back to that wedding certificate and the revelations it provided.

He *had* to get married, our Geordie did. His first child, Elsie, was born in August 1912. It is probably only my generation that can still feel some echo of the shock and horror that the phrase 'had to get married' could provoke – and that all came from our parents. And once you were married, then no matter how miserable the two people were and how unsuited, joyless and loveless the relationship might become, you would never *ever* divorce even though every day was like the Field Punishment Number One I mentioned earlier.

Aye son, that's true enough like.

In the mid 1980s I worked as a carer in an Old People's Home in Wiltshire, at the time when the Social Services were clearing out the long term casualties of the ancient and crumbling Mental Hospitals. Two of the very elderly women who came to us had spent their entire lives in what had originally been termed a Lunatic Asylum, for no other reason than that they had been unmarried mothers. "Oi never did nobody no harm, honest!" said little Veronica, crying when I let her cuddle my own first baby. I held her hand when she died, still pining for the one that had been taken away from her at about the time George and Jane got married.

In 1912, getting pregnant and not being married was almost a crime against humanity – and don't fool yourselves that the noble working classes had a healthier attitude toward such things than the posh lot doon Sooth. Not in Ashington they didn't. Even in the mid-1960s when a young lad living in our street 'had to get married' there was much embarrassment and an awful lot of whispering and I remember him walking to the shops, head bent low and not meeting anyone's eyes, but at least avoiding the dog shit on the way.

Our Geordie had to get married, and he did, but why would he lie about his age? Why claim to be 27 when he was 30?

Personally I think 30 would have been a very difficult age for him. He was a simple barman with no education and no prospects. All the hopes he had of playing centre forward for Newcastle United and England had been flushed doon the koondy.[19] He would never, now, be able to afford one of them Model T Fords or even just a 'Modèle De Luxe' Light Roadster bicycle that he drooled over in the catalogues. Plus his father-in-law to be, the very tough John Yellowley who hewed coal for a living, didn't think much of him at all. *A barman? Eh? What kinda job is that Jinny?* he would have asked his daughter when he first learned about her beau.

Nowadays we think of 60 as the new 50 (and I keep telling myself that), or say 30 is the new 20. But in 1912, with poor nutrition and

---

19 Gutter, storm drain

the very poor general health of the working class population, then we might say that 30 was more like our 50, and there were no self-help magazines then which would ever change that attitude.

So I'm telling you, with absolute certainty, that at the age of 30 George Matthew Richardson felt such a failure that he lied about his age both to his Jane Yellowley, his new in-laws, and all of the children whom he later created.

By the time that War was declared on 4th Aug 1914, his daughter Elsie was 2 and my own Dad was nearly 1 year old. It is quite possible that there was another one on the way, but I haven't yet checked the dates for little May, who died as an infant.

Two questions arise from this:
Did the ordinary people have any idea that war was brewing?
Why did Geordie, with at least two children at home, enlist?
Once we answer these, we can get our avatar lowpin'[20] across to France – though believe you me, hinnies, we won't be doing him any favours...

To answer the first question, yes Geordie knew. He was a barman. He got newspapers in the Hotel for the guests and read them first, and then gave them to Jinny to take up, probably preceded by a whispered: *Owt gannin, pet?*[21] before she gave him a quick snog in the cellars and went about her work, glowing.

The *Newcastle Journal, Evening Chronicle* and local *Morpeth Herald* (which is the only one that finally honoured him) would have given news about Churchill enlarging the Royal Navy and removing the fleet from Malta back to home waters, with the French doing similar.

---

20 Jumping. Sexual activity among the Geordies might be described as 'geet lowpin's in the neet'.
21 *Anything going, pet?* i.e. of a romantic and preferably sexual nature without her scary Dad being told.

He would have seen comments in every edition about the German expansion of both her navy and her land armies, which saw rising numbers of battleships and cruisers being built, and the German Army increased from 136,000 to 760,908. It would have seemed that almost every issue of the *Daily Mail* was commenting on how our country had become soft, and that we were having picnic on the edge of a volcano, and that we jolly well needed to wake up and take up arms.

There were small wars in middle Europe when Austria-Hungary engaged in conflict with Serbia, constant tension between the French and Germans which led to Lord Haldane warning the German Ambassador that England would aid France if attacked by Germany: Britain could not allow the balance of power to be changed.

By November of 1912 King Albert of Belgium was invited to Berlin to try and broker some kind of peace, but the Kaiser told the King that he felt war with France was inevitable.

As Geordie would also be aware, that 'balance of power' which His Majesty the King-Emperor of Britain sought to maintain was as much to do with preserving the status quo within his own citizens as anything more global.

The period 1911-1914 had the lowest level of unemployment since 1901, thanks to the power of coal and steam, and places like Armstrong's Factories, yet real wages were not rising and up to a third of the population was on or below the poverty line. Almost a third of men who volunteered for the Army in 1909-10 were rejected on grounds of ill-health. We've already seen what the infant mortality rate was like in that area.

The Liverpool General Transport Strike of 1911 caused tremors within the hierarchies. It involved dockers, railway workers, sailors and people from a host of other trades. Liverpool commerce was paralysed for most of the summer. If that could happen in one town, what might happen if the rot spread?

There were 41 million working days lost to strikes in 1912. Most of them were treated with a weary but wary tolerance. But the miners' strikes of that year made the ruling classes very worried indeed. If the coal stopped being mined then every factory would have to close. The nation was utterly dependent on those filthy men digging out that filthy but utterly necessary substance. There was no way to beat the strike, as coal-mining by soldiers or inexperienced labourers was out of the question. And there was not a trace of what those union chappies called blacklegging. In five days a new law was rushed through Parliament which introduced a minimum wage, and reduced working hours.

As the rapscallion signing himself V.I. Lenin wrote: 'The workers have learned to fight. They have come to see the path that will lead them to victory. They have become aware of their strength. They have ceased to be the meek lambs they seemed to be for so long a time, to the joy of all the defenders and extollers of wage-slavery.'[22]

The suffragettes at the time, showing enormous and unyielding courage, were bent on attacking every sacred British cow in their urge to be given the vote. Initial amusement at their antics turned to total shock at seeing respectable women smashing windows, burning down pavilions, defacing cricket pitches, golf courses and Gentlemen's Clubs, going on hunger strikes and causing the equivalent of millions of pounds worth of damage across the nation. They used little hammers hidden in their muffs, and caused as much damage to the British status quo as the footsoldiers with their own hammers did to French chivalry at Agincourt.

I don't think any Northumbrian would have been too surprised when those women showed their power. There is even a legend of a Geordie woman who disguised herself as a man and enlisted in the Northumberland Fusiliers in the early 19th Century to keep near her beau. She fought a few good battles therein before she was discovered. That proud northerner and Yorkshireman Sir Michael Parkinson once commented: "We're all frightened of our women up there." Further up in Northumberland, in the *real* north-east, a million men would have nodded ruefully.

And as for the Troubles in Ireland, and all the agitations that had started there… Oh dear god but that's still going yet.

Geordie's and Geordies' own politics were complicated issues and certainly in my Dad's case were firmly toward what is now being called 'Blue Labour'. And if I have to raise my own colours these days as a 'Red Conservative' who would take the bullet for dear Queenie, then a detour into these areas would take too long and be too confusing. The only truly black and white thing in that area is to be found in the football strip.

---

22 Pravda No. 1, January 1, 1913

Reading the letters to one of his three sons 30 years later, Wor Geordie comes across very strongly as a clever man with enough confidence in his literary skills to express a 'voice'. He would have skimmed over all the daily newspapers and many more, while as a barman he was always speaking to travellers and businessmen who were at least tangentially connected to the greater events of the day. In my day the Grand Hotel was just a down-beat pub that very old men and the burgeoning drug dealers would frequent. No-one ever stayed the night there, or in either of the two other 'hotels' in town. In his day however, long before the coal mines were nationalised, the rich mine owners and their business partners would have seen this as the first port call if they wanted to stay overnight. In its early days, it was the Ritz and Savoy and the Park Lane rolled into one.

And in ways that no-one else in Ashington could match, he had his finger on the international pulse.

Eh?

In the post-Mam years when I visited Ashington, Dad and I still hadn't learned to communicate properly and – sadly – never did. But we had companionable silences watching the telly (625 lines black and white, given by Wor Pat) which he insisted on watching with no other room lights on, as he reckoned it would give a better picture. It drove me mad and gave me a thumping heid, but I went along with it because we shared the same taste in co'boys. His argument: *There's nae such thing as a bad co'boy* is infallible, and even today I bow to no-one in my belief that *The Outlaw Josey Wales* is the best co'boy fillum ever made.

On this occasion however we were actually watching *Starsky and Hutch,* those tough New York 'carps' who wouldn't have lasted two minutes doon the pits. It was their most difficult case yet. A crack team of renegade and highly trained assassins were at loose within the city and were going to murder the visiting Russian president. This could tip America into a devastating nuclear war. Their mission, should they choose to iron their flares and accept it, was to find the mono-browed villains with their Russo-Brooklyn accents and save the world.

So how did they find these ultra-professional elite killers? As always they went to the local bar and pool hall where the all-knowing and rather sinister proprietor Huggy Bear muttered: *The woid on the street is…*

Whadda loada of kack, we said and switched over to watch the equally sinister Hughie Green instead.

'Woid'? What the hell's that?
Ah Dad man, it means 'word' to rhyme with 'turd'. But you'd pronounce 'word' to rhyme with 'cord'. Can I just tell me story?
Ah jist wish ye'd get started.

The point is, the workers in Armstrong's factory could have told anyone who cared to listen that a great big war was a-coming. Geordie would have guessed this himself even years earlier when he worked there as a machinist, and he would have kept up with all the gossip since from his dad and his siblings. The workers there might not understand the intricacies and the alliances of the global politics (who does?) but they could count: From making *x* number of shells in the factories in 1905 they were now making *xxxxx* – millions of the buggers, no end in sight. *Whey man it was obvious.*

Across the Scotswood Road, on the Tyne itself, there were Armstrong warships springing up and squelching out of every dock: HMSs Monarch, Canada, Agincourt, Erin, Malaya and Eagle.

And then there were the aircraft, the funny looking FK1 which never got very far, and the more useful FK3[23] (and you can imagine the fun they had with *those* names), and there was wondering talk about how some aeroplanes had definitely been fitted with guns, and some of them could do varnigh[24] 100 miles an hoor.

By the end of the war Armstrong's factory would claim to have built 102 tanks, 13,000 guns, 12,000 gun carriages, 109 warships, 230 merchant ships, 15 million shells, 21 million cartridge cases and 18 million fuses.

During this period the inventors and engineers were constantly improving the fire-power and effectiveness of their machine-guns in particular, to get one up on the Germans with their nasty Maxim guns.

Generals Haig and French down in London would never have given this particular output much support because they felt that rifles and machine-guns couldn't possibly prevail against a boldly executed cavalry charge.

---

[23] The first pilots in the Royal Flying Corps had to be officers from reputable public schools. They also had be excellent horsemen, or they would not be considered for training.
[24] nearly

The engineers in Geordies' factories knew better.

The ordinary folk in his family didn't have phones then, but with four postal deliveries every day, his dad, siblings and cousins could write to him in the morning with the gossip and get a reply by the afternoon of the same day. It wouldn't be so much the word on the street that gave the secrets, but the word from the assembly lines.

The German General Staff had produced the Schlieffen Plan for the invasion of France, through Belgium, as early as 1905. The fact is, everyone knew that war was coming even if the common man didn't fully understand the international claims and tensions. They even coined the term 'Great War' before that first shot was fired. For years it had been a rough beast slouching not toward Bethlehem as Yeats' poem had it, but westward toward Flanders, dragging all sorts of horror with it, and churning up the mud and the national psyches as no beast had ever done before.

I don't even begin to understand it myself, and certainly couldn't begin to apportion blame to any one country even though all the world's fingers tended to point toward Germany. The truth is, they all seemed to be spoiling for a fight. Perhaps because, as at the time of Agincourt, they knew that the common men would do all the hard work and the hard dying, and they would make what profit out of the carnage they could. If nothing else, a jolly good war would take their minds off all these dangerously worrying socialist ideas.[25]

When the Archduke Franz Ferdinand of Austria was assassinated by a Serbian nationalist student, Gavrilo Princip, on 28th July 1914 it was (apparently) inevitable that Austria declared war on Serbia, though I can't for the life of me see that even now, surrounded as I am by books about the time. The average Tommy had no interest in the archduke. His death was a matter of supreme disinterest. Their simple understanding of the war was that this new-formed nation called Germany[26] was sweeping across Europe, aiming toward the Channel ports, devastating poor but plucky Belgium, and likely to

---

25 It worked. In 1916 only 2.5 million working days were lost to strikes in Britain, as opposed to 20 times that many four years before.
26 Germany became a unified nation in 1871.

bring down the British Empire itself if these German chappies were not stopped.

And from that single shot, fired in a place that neither me nor Geordie could confidently point to on a map, it was like the Greyhound Races at Portland Park when all the dogs exploded from their traps and set off running hell for leather, throwing up the dirt with their paws, slavering with blood-lust in pursuit of a hare that wasn't even real.

Russia mobilised and through their alliance with France, called on the French to mobilise.

On 1 Aug 1914 Germany declared war on Russia

On 3 Aug 1914 Germany declared war on France and her troops poured into neutral Belgium as directed under the Schlieffen Plan, drawn up seven years earlier.

This is what the French and British elite had yearned for. Infringing the neutrality of dear little peace-loving Belgium was their means of being able to declare a Just War. And by jingo they certainly needed a Just War in order to stop the socialist rot which threatened to topple monarchies everywhere. From that moment onward the Germans became Huns.

The British foreign secretary, Sir Edward Grey, sent an ultimatum to Germany demanding their withdrawal from Belgium where the Germans were – everyone was told – committing the most awful atrocities.

In his book published in 1915, *Belgium in War-Time*, Commandant de Gerlache de Gommery goes into as much detail as modern taste and censorship would allow regarding the German actions. His list is apparently endless, and he asserts that he witnessed even more dreadful events that he could not begin to describe. A few paragraphs plucked at random:

> German artillerymen firing upon the Carmelite convent at Chevremont secured themselves against the fire of the fort by placing all round their battery men, and even women and children, captured in the neighbourhood...
>
> In very many parts of Hainault the Germans forced civilians, men and women, to precede or accompany them. Thus a German column passing through Marchienne drove before it a group of several hundreds of civilians; it was marching upon Montigny-le-Tilleul, where the first important engagement with the French took place...

> The German troops who entered Tournai on the 24th of August were preceded by several ranks of civilians. I might give many more such examples...
>
> On the 5th of August, about 2 o'clock in the afternoon, some German troops, repulsed and thrown into confusion by the fire of the Fleron fort, entered Soumagne, a large village of 4,750 inhabitants. "It's your brothers who are firing on us from the forts!" they cried. "We are going to take our revenge!" They arrested a hundred of the inhabitants, led them into a meadow, and there killed them by rifle-bullet or bayonet. The village was partially burned.
>
> In the list of 105 victims I find the names of a baby of eleven months, a little boy of three years, a girl of thirteen, and several aged persons of either sex.

The influential *The War Illustrated* carried a headline on 5th September 1914 entitled 'Horrible Stories of German Fiendishness' which recounted how their correspondents in Belgium had seen little murdered children with roasted feet, the tiny mites having been hung over a fire before they were slain.

Call me old-fashioned if you like but there would have been something wrong with Geordie if he *didn't* want to do his bit after having read about Germans bayoneting babies, raping any woman in Belgium who had a pulse and shooting coal miners. The whole of Ashington would have been up in arms.

Did he really believe all the propaganda?

In the early days, probably yes. This was in an era of innocence when people thought that if it was in a newspaper it must be true. Later on I used to think the same about the BBC. Wars might be stupid and banal, expressions of the purest evil, but men like Geordie can also want to fight in them for the best of motives. And it does seem that while the German misdeeds were given a great deal of 'spin' for propaganda purposes, their Army really did do a lot of very dark and ruthless things to the Belgian civilians. At very least, demonising them as Huns would do no harm when it came to mobilising the British civilians for war.

> *He nivver spoke badly aboot the Jarmins he fought though.*

He never demonised them?

> *Ner. The only demon in wor hoose, according tae me Mam, waz him.*

It was Light against Darkness right from the start. So on 4th August 1914, with an apparent show of great reluctance and only operating out of the highest motives, but knowing that they had the whole country behind them in often unexpected ways and at unexpected levels, Britain declared war on Germany.

I would imagine that the cheers from the colliery rows in Ashington were heard along the Pall Mall.

Which leaves now the second question. Given that he had a wife and children to support, and the fact that conscription had not yet been introduced, why did Geordie enlist? I think there were other things going on within his heart and mind just then in that summer of 1914.

First there was the financial aspect. In 1914 the average coal miner was taking home 5/9d for a 58-hour week.[27] As a barman, he can't have been earning that much.

Since the Defence of the Realm Act had come into force in August 1914 the pub opening hours had been restricted to 12 noon–2:30 p.m. and 6:30 p.m.–9:30 p.m., which would have had a huge effect on his own earnings.

In contrast, one of his contemporaries in the Fusiliers recorded that, as soldiers, they were able to send back to their families 6d per day (3/6 per week), with the government adding another 9/0, making 12/6 per week payable to wives and mothers back home.

So in that respect he could leave them and not feel too guilty.

Secondly, there was pressure on all able-bodied men to answer Lord Kitchener's call of 'Your Country Needs You'. These formed part of what became known as the New Army, and there was huge response. Almost 2.5 million men volunteered.

There is a picture of Company Sergeant Major Charlton recruiting for the 4th Northumberland Fusiliers at Christmas 1915. He's got 16 in all. A couple on the front row look rather desperate. It is very likely that Grandad would have known these people. CSM Charlton would have been fêted by the young 'uns at the time like

---

27 For those young 'uns who don't know the old money, this really wasn't very much.

a modern rock star, but I can't help thinking he was more like the Child Snatcher in *Chitty Chitty Bang Bang*.

Unlike France and Germany, who had been preparing and building their armies for years, conscription in Britain didn't come into place until the 2nd of March 1916. After that time men could no longer choose which regiment they entered, and could be sent anywhere. Before that all the pressure came from the accusing finger of Lord Kitchener which pointed out to everyone who saw it that their country needed THEM. His appeal was so potent that five New Armies were created, and numbered K1 to K5.

On top of that pressure, Lord Derby and Sir Henry Rawlinson hit upon the idea of battalions (usually about 1000 men) formed from like-minded locals. If men knew they could serve with their chums, they might be more likely to enlist. Hence the appearance of the Pals Battalions with names like the Grimsby Chums, Artists' Rifles, Accrington Pals, Newcastle Commercials, etc.

During this crucial recruiting period there were active groups of women, members of the Organisation of the White Feather, handing out white feathers of cowardice to those whom they suspected were shirking their duty. Even soldiers home on leave – and out of uniform – found themselves the (disgusted) target of bearers of white feathers.

Newspapers like the Hexham Courant for example, joined in by showing a front page picture of six young men from Allendale who had joined the Northumberland Fusiliers, and said in huge letters under them:

THESE BOYS DIDN'T SHIRK
THEY WANT HELP!! Listen for a moment.
Can't you hear them calling TO YOU?
BE A MAN.
There's a King's uniform waiting for YOU.
Go and put it on NOW.

GOD SAVE THE KING!

The pressure from all sides was enormous, and it would have taken a brave man indeed to say to them all the immortal battle-phrase *Haddaway an' Shite* and just carry on as normal, because he never could.

The government didn't have to push too hard. The lines of Geordies eager to enlist stretched right around St George's Drill Hall in Newcastle; it had to stay open all night. They used football matches, theatres and cinemas as recruiting grounds. They pulled in the volunteers at Gosforth Races and the Blaydon Races themselves, usually with bands playing. It's very hard not to march to the beat of a big drum especially if your mates were already doing so.

By the January of 1916 two and a half million men had enlisted, though it was noted that the working classes had not shown quite the same levels of zeal as those above. Though as my Dad once pointed out, it's easier to be adventurous and take risks as a young man when you've got money in the bank or a wealthy and doting Mam. Otherwise, if you got work, you stuck to it like a limpet on the rocks doon at Newbiggin.

The danger that peace might break out instead because of the international socialist bonds of the workers just faded overnight. German socialists fell back upon their *völkisch*[28] roots and wanted to crush the Russian Imperialists on their eastern borders. The Russian socialists had had enough of German militarism and capitalism and suddenly wanted to destroy the cause of all their problems – the Kaiser – and get back to global amity later. The British socialists were so appalled by the plight of the poor, peaceful but plucky Belgian underdogs that they wanted to get stuck in on their behalf. And the French socialists, ambivalent and bewildering as ever, became so enamoured of their need to cleave toward *la patrie* instead of solidarity that they enlisted in massive numbers, and you just couldn't stop them singing *La Marseillaise* all that summer.

This is all well beyond our experience now, in the relatively safe haven of the 21st Century and perhaps not easy to understand. After all, in February 2003 an estimated one million people (some say nearly twice that) protested against Prime Minister Tony Blair's illegal war in Iraq, and at least something of this was to do with the cannon-fire of the Somme which still whooshed and banged down the strands of their DNA.

That echo was particularly strong when the Geordies went to war again in 1940 and the streets of Newcastle were filled not with the cheering, adoring masses of 1914, but with deathly silent people

---

28 A complex of meanings involving, blood, soil, race and ancestors.

who knew what war was *really* about, compelling one of the young Fusiliers to stand up on a wagon and cry out:

"Ah howay man ye miserable lot… We're not deid yit!"

But in 1914 it was not simply a question of blood lust which caused such a fervour. Many confirmed and utterly brave pacifists at the time observed that they also felt themselves being swirled toward the vortex of patriotism. When it comes down to it, when that whistle blows, people become tribal.

Many years ago when I was a young man in America, imagining I was Ashington's answer to Jack Kerouac, the onset of the Falklands War between Britain and Argentina caused me a deep agony: I *had* to get back. I *had* to be on English soil while this was going on. There was nothing I could actually do once I got there, and I would have been, as The Mam might have observed of me also, 'as much use a nick in a coo's arse'. The pull was illogical, derisory but utterly irresistible. I got the next flight home.[29]

All of this would have been going on in Geordie's head and heart too, and in many ways the War would have seemed to him as much of a godsend as it was to higher echelons of British society and industry. After all, everyone said it would be a quick little skirmish, and certainly over by Christmas. There were the financial aspects mentioned earlier whereby he'd be able to send more money back to his family than he could ever earn in the Grand Hotel. Plus he had seen his young brother William go off to America and do bold things there and he would have felt huge envy.[30]

And finally, although he loved his bairns, his wife Jinny was – how would you say this? – somewhat er, difficult at times. My Mam, her unfavoured daughter-in-law, expressed it rather more forcefully than that. And my older sister Pat, who saw a lot of her in action, fully agreed.

Ye knaa Alan, the way Francey acted tae me was exactly like the way me Mam acted tae me Dad.

---

[29] Though no-one else knew I was returning, Dad knew the moment I touched British soil and told a friend: *Wor Alan's home noo.*
[30] He joined the US Army and fought in France.

It's a common thing. Men often marry their mothers in that respect.

Aye, but Aah wazn't clivver at that trick-cycling stuff of yours.

She demonised you Dad. You didn't deserve it.

Divvn't marry your Mam, Alan, whativver ye dae.

In fact I did. But she gave me four wonderful daughters and eventually set me free, so I cannot complain. Although I was fully aware of the psychology behind the idea that we often marry our own parents, there were times when I seriously wondered whether my ex-wife was actually being possessed by my Mam. I mean this literally. My ex was in a routine of speaking to me and treating me exactly as Mam had done to Dad, though without the physical violence. It was uncanny. Even as this was going on, I had a dim sense that this too was a second generation echo of how Granny Jinny had related to Grandad Richison – Wor Geordie – perhaps punishing him for his odd behaviour when he came back from Flanders. Or did Dad's broken watch send out vibrations which made my wife and myself respond like tuning forks, 80 years later? I think not, but I clutched at straws like this to explain it all.

However, had he known this in advance it wouldn't have stopped Wor Geordie going to battle in the first place. He was 32 when war was declared and life was passing him by. For once, he wanted some adventure. Danger? He'd be safe within his tribe. Once again we get back to the Northumbrian attitude:

Howay man hinny...[31] *What chance would them Jarmins an' their daft spiky hats stand against a bunch o' hard Geordie lads, eh?*

There was even a joke about this, which spread like wildfire, and which will lead on to the history and tone of the regiment in due course. The story goes:

A regiment of Prussians was marching along the road toward Wipers, hundreds of the buggers, Imperial Guards.

Suddenly, Geordie appears in the doorway of a ruined church, no hat, no gun.

"Think yer hard Fritzie?" he spits out to their Colonel, and rolls up his sleeves. "I'll tek yiz all on, six at a time."

Whey, the Jarmins roared with laughter, didn't they? The Colonel, who liked ter see a bit of spirit in an enemy, sent six of his toughest lads into the church. There was an aalmighty clattering

---

31 Loosely translated as: *Oh come on pal...* (Said with emphasis!)

and a few screams before Geordie appears in the doorway, bloodied but unbowed, and caalls oot: "Whae's next?"

So the Colonel, angry by this time, sends up another six. Same result. The Colonel is stottin' up and doon by noo and he sends ten of his very best men tae deal with this Geordie creature, and after another aalmighty battle one of them eventually staggers oot, covered in blood, hardly able to stand, and cries:

"Mein Gott! It's a trap – there's TWO of them. RUN!!!"

Which leaves us with another quality to energise our avatar with before he finally gets put into uniform.

Y'see if there was one thing that really preyed on Geordie's mind and occupied his passions every bit as much as job, marras and family, plus the excitement and fear of what was ahead for him in the Army, it was the information contained in this table for the 1913-14 Football Season:

Newcastle United 1913-1914
English Division One

		P	GA	Pt	Home Res	Away Res
1	Blackburn Rovers	38	1.86	51	D0-0	L0-3
2	Aston Villa	38	1.30	44	D2-2	W3-1
3	Middlesbrough	38	1.28	43	W1-0	L0-3
4	Oldham Athletic	38	1.22	43	D0-0	L0-3
5	West Bromwich Albion	38	1.09	43	D3-3	D1-1
6	Bolton Wanderers	38	1.25	42	W4-3	L1-3
7	**Sunderland**	38	1.21	40	W2-1	W2-1
8	Chelsea	38	0.84	39	W1-0	W1-0
9	Bradford City	38	1.00	38	D0-0	L0-2
10	Sheffield United	38	1.05	37	W2-1	L0-2
11	**Newcastle United**	38	0.81	37		
12	Burnley	38	1.15	36	W3-1	L0-1
13	Manchester City	38	0.96	36	L0-1	W1-0
14	Manchester United	38	0.84	36	L0-1	D2-2
15	Everton	38	0.84	35	L0-1	L0-2

16 Liverpool	38	0.74	35	L1-2	D0-0
17 Tottenham Hotspur	38	0.81	34	W2-0	D0-0
18 Sheffield Wednesday	38	0.76	34	W3-1	D0-0
19 Preston North End	38	0.75	30	W2-0	L1-4
20 Derby County	38	0.78	27	D1-1	L0-2

2 points for a win
Goal average applies when teams are level on points

True Believers, i.e. Newcastle United supporters, will understand the shocking significance of this table at once and need no further comment. Please lads, sit doon, put yer heids between yer knees and tayk deep breaths. During this research I also found out something so shameful that I've had to tuck it away in the back of this book as Appendix 4.

I'm not being crass. Supporting Newcastle United has been for most Geordies something akin to a long drawn out Near Death Experience, often feeling that we're going down a long tunnel to nowhere, but unable to resist the Great Light that seems to be promised at the far end. Make no mistake I was totally useless at playing the game and was more Walter, Prince of Softies than Alan Shearer. I never *wanted* to support them and there have been times without number when I've sworn never to watch them again, but... in the worst times of my life I've still found the urge to look up the football results and see how they've done.

And that table above is important as being something of a milestone.

When the final whistle blew to end the last match of the 1913-1914 season those early superstars went back into the little shed that served as a changing room, scraped the mud off their own boots, stripped and washed themselves clean at the communal sink, using as much of the green carbolic soap provided as they wanted. They got dressed, wrapped their kit in their wet towels, combed and parted their hair precisely, put on their cloth caps and made their individual ways home. Some of them walked, because they lived that near; others, from the south side of the Tyne, caught buses along with their own supporters.

There were no Maseratis or personal helicopters. No Wags waiting for them. No agents negotiating 7-figure weekly wages or transfers to 'bigger' clubs. This was decades before the evolution of those mysterious ailments which ensured that some modern-day Newcastle players seemed to spend more time on the treatment tables, or spending their leisure with their race horses, or on the pull down the Quayside discos, or becoming Kings of Bling rather than shimmying their hips and scoring goals before their worshipping fans on the hallowed sward of St James' Park.

But Alan, ye canna blame them for the big wages.
I don't Dad, it's all them groin strains they seem to get.
Oh aye...they wazn't invented in my day. Nor substitutes.

No, this lot got home and ate their fish and chips (with batter scrapin's), or maybe a couple of pease pudding sandwiches, puffed away on a nice relaxing cigarette and then without any fuss or publicity put their cloth caps on again and walked to their local recruitment centres and enlisted. Most of them, including two Newcastle United directors, the team doctor, and all the young ground staff joined the Northumberland Fusiliers.

Getting into Europe had never been easier for *that* Newcastle team.

The next (and for some of them the last) time they would kick a football again in earnest after hearing a whistle blow would be in a little place in France called Thiepval, where half of them were massacred.

Listen... If you want to understand Big Geordie (or any Geordie) you have to accept the deep-rooted passion that he would have taken with him to the Western Front, shared by almost all of his mates. It was not so much a love which dare not speak its name, but a love which felt compelled to shout it to everyone, at every opportunity, compressed into the tribal and irresistible cry of: *Howay the Lads!* I'll bet anything a few of them went over the top shouting exactly that – and I hope to god they came back.

Ashington at that time and for many decades after was – quite literally on some levels – like one of those Black Holes which exist in interstellar space, with dark gravities sucking everything into it.

It was said in Geordie's era that there were in fact four roads by which you could escape the town.

Eh? you were supposed to say, because there were quite clearly only three. Ashington was built around a kind of tau-cross of roads, with the Grand Hotel at the junction where the three roads met and all the gadgies like me Dad would lean against the railings and put the world to rights. There was the road east toward Newbiggin by the Sea, and the once golden beaches and the willicks[32] you could pick from the rocks. There was the road west toward the slightly posh Morpeth and its lovely promenade which curves lazily along the River Wansbeck. There was the road directly south which eventually led to the Holy City, some 20 miles away.

So where's this bliddy fourth road then? you were then meant to ask.

And the answer would crash into the back of your net like a ball hit on the volley: Football.

When Geordie Richison died, at 69 Alexandra Road, he could have looked out of the back window across to the fields of the Welfare and seen the very young and blond Bobby Charlton kicking the ball around with his older brother Jack, both of whom went on to win the World Cup in 1966. He, who had been a true hero in a brutal war, listened intently and excitedly on the steam radio to details of this cracking new lad Newcastle had signed called Jackie Milburn (second cousin to the Charlton brothers). Although this was during World War 2, and Milburn had to work down the mines under the same terms as Dad, he managed to appear for Newcastle United in Wartime League games from 1943 onward and became a scoring legend.

If you had the skill, then football could get you out of the pits, but nothing else.[33]

Well, that's what I thought, because when I looked more closely at the main Medal Card and did just a tiny bit of extra research, I realised that when the War was declared Geordie had already found his own fourth road.

This one kept him well out of the pits, gave him a huge sense of dignity and that bit of extra money he was always needing, and at the age of 33 stopped him from beginning to feel that he was of use to neither man nor beast.

He was a member of the Territorials.

---

32 winkles
33 There is now a large bronze statue to Jackie Milburn in Ashington town centre.

5

BEHIND THE LINES

THE FIRST Medal Card I got from the National Archives showed that *Richardson, G.M., Regimental Number 4214* was a private in the 6th Battalion Northumberland Fusiliers. T.F. which means Territorial Force.

In 1908 the army reforms carried out by the Minister of War, Richard Haldane, did away with the old, local part-time military units known as the Militia and the Volunteers and replaced them with the Territorial Force. It was essentially a form of part-time soldiering – the 'Saturday Night Soldiers' – whose primary role was that of home defence. They were not obliged to serve overseas, although in practice they almost all did. And if they were called into full-time service, usually lasting four years, their jobs would still be held open for them on their return.

The Territorials were separated into First and Second Line Units. Those men who did not agree to serve overseas were placed in 'Home Service' or 'Second Line' units. Those who did agree became known as 'Foreign Service' or 'First Line'.

Geordie agreed to do so. He may have been a member of the TF before war was declared and as we have seen was as likely to have been as excited about it as anyone in the higher stratospheres doon in London.

The Territorial Force still exists today, and with much the same role, although it is now known as an Army rather than a Force. The TF or TA was/is never a soft option. I have spoken to a Territorial member of the SAS who pointed out that they have full SAS training and have to pass all the extreme criteria while still doing a full-time job in the real world.

When I started this book I had assumed that Geordie had been sucked into the war and was a victim, driven toward the slaughter like a sacrificial lamb.

Sadly, tellingly, when the French *poilus*[34] were being marched along the Voie Sacrée to a slaughter-field at Verdun that was every bit as incomprehensible as that of the Somme, some of the braver or more nervous soldiers made the noise of sheep. The whole strategy of the British Somme Offensive was to relieve the pressure on the French at Verdun – that green hill not too far away from them, but which had no city walls left at all because of the unrelenting German shelling.

Yet the more I learned about him, the more I realised that he went into it with his eyes wide open, and probably spent his last night buying everyone pints at The Grand.

When Geordies' War was declared the Territorial battalions were numbered on after those of the Regular Army and Special Reserve. The latter was a form of part-time soldiering similar to the Territorial Force. Men would enlist into the Special Reserve for 6 years and had to accept the possibility of being called up in the event of a war and undertake all the same conditions as men of the Army Reserve.

The new organisation, as part of the Northumbrian Division, later entitled 50th (Northumbrian) Division was thus:

- 1st Battalion
- 2nd Battalion
- 3rd Battalion (Special Reserve)
- 4th Battalion (T.F.) (HQ Hexham, from bulk of 1st V.B.[35])
- 5th Battalion (T.F.) (HQ Walker, redesignation of 2nd V.B.)
- 6th (City) Battalion (T.F.) (HQ Newcastle, redesignation of 3rd V.B.)
- 7th Battalion (T.F.) (HQ Alnwick, from part of 1st V.B.)
- 8th (Cyclist) Battalion (redesignated Northern Cyclist Battalion and transferred to Army Cyclist Corps 1915)[36]

---

34 Literally 'Hairy Ones' – their equivalent of the term Tommy.
35 Volunteer Battalion
36 They were based for a time behind Woodhorn Colliery, on the northern edge of Ashington.

The notion of the Cyclist Battalions creates an almost risible image in our minds today but they were serious machines, easy to maintain, and in some terrains faster than horses. The idea was that cyclists would act as high-speed messengers between different points of the battlefield. In reality, because they could neither move in the mud nor drive their machines through the trenches, they all became infantrymen.

Exactly the same fate befell the elite cavalry that Haig had placed so much faith in.

As I pondered all this a phrase kept flickering into my mind, half formed, which muttered 'A man without history is like... like...' I couldn't remember the rest. I googled those words and it took me to Marcus Garvey's comment: "A people without the knowledge of their past history, origin and culture is like a tree without roots."

Immediately under that single quote was a large advert on the website which said:

The Territorial Army
Get paid to be a soldier in Your spare time. Recruiting now.
Army.Mod.uk/TerritorialArmy

I suppose Grandad was trying to tell me something.

It was inevitable that he would join the Northumberland Fusiliers. If we now have to give our Geordie avatar some sort of attitude to get it gannin', then we must look to the history of the regiment he was so proud to join even if, as Ambrose Bierce commented wickedly: 'History is an account, mostly false, of events, mostly unimportant, which are brought about by rulers, mostly knaves, and soldiers, mostly fools.'

The stories of soldiers, as told by soldiers, are pretty much one-sided and just as dodgy as those told by Mams and Dads – and I include myself in that ignoble consideration.

I remember once, when I was 7, seeing Mam sitting on the edge of the bed and looking at Dad's Watch. She must have made a routine inspection of all his hidey holes. I think that was probably the first time I had seen it. She'd taken the net curtains down to wash and their spaces were filled with single large pages of the Newcastle Journal, hung on the taut wires that held the nets.

The sun bleezed through the print and the pictures. There was a big photo, sideyways, of the Munich Air Disaster when half of the Manchester United team had been killed. The house smelled of ironing and the rather acrid tang of Omo washing powder, and warmth crept upstairs from all the pots and pans of boiling water on the big open fire in the kitchen.

She held the watch out toward me.

"He was a canny bit lad," she said, her ultimate accolade, and I thought for a moment she might have talking about my Dad, as the names were the same. There was a long silence. She looked into the golden disk as if she were scrying the past in it and all the might-have-beens in her own embattled life. "He used tae come aroond and have a cuppa tea."

Grandad Richison was a very sad man, she explained, although I didn't realise there was anything that needed explaining. He was very quiet, she said quietly; he got a lot of grief from his bliddy aaful wife, she told me, who had given grief to everyone close.

I saw him in my mind's eye as I saw everything (and still do) on a little cinema screen before my brow, slightly to the left and about 6" by 4". He did seem lost – seemed quiet and lost and in pain.

"Yer fatha nivver spoke tae him," said Mam. "They nivver taalked."

I looked at the inscription and was impressed. "Us Richisons must be brave, Mam," I ventured.

She snorted in that guttural way that posh people might write up as Bah! If only you knew! She was not a Richison!

Then she told me that when Grandad was being awarded this stupid little watch by the people of Ashington, her cousin Billy Kinghorn was oot in Russia, getting himself intae a bit o' trouble with one o' them Rohmanov lassies. The revolutionaries thowt he was a spy and put him up against a waall ter shoot him. Tha fingers were on the triggers and he was varnigh a gonner until he saved himself by crying oot the immortal words:

"Lads, lads, howay man! Put yer guns doon. Ah'm not a spy, Ah'm from Whitley Bay!"

That was real and true heroism in her eyes. What did the Richisons ivver do for her?

Billy Kinghorn? Ah've nivver heord of him.
Nor me, Dad. I've tried to track him down too, but with no luck.
Ah think she was maykin' that one up. She did that ye knaa.
I know, but that's too stupid not to be true.

He gave a guttural snort in my head just like The Mam's.[37]

The Northumberland Fusiliers were originally known as the Irish Regiment in 1674 and even then bore the badge of St George and the Dragon. Its motto was *Quo Fata Vocant* – 'Whither the Fates call'. I'm not quite sure what that meant.

Gan where yer told, son. Divvin't complain. Divvin't explain.
What, like them poilus at Verdun going baa?
Whey, aalright, mebbe more like them present day footballers: It means ti them 'Grab what ye can when ye can'. It's a short life son, ye canna blame anybody for that.

When the regiment distinguished themselves for the first time in battle at the Siege of Maastricht the pitifully grateful Prince of Orange gave them a gift of six sheep and a very fat ox and you can almost see the fat bastard whimpering with relief.

They quickly gained such a reputation for derring-do and elan that they were nicknamed 'The Old and Bold', and much later 'Lord Wellington's Bodyguard' and even 'The Shiners' when they were in Ireland, as a testament to the cleanliness and smartness of the regiment. But when they were transferred to the British Service on 5th June 1685, establishing its order of precedence as the 5th Regiment of the Line, they became known as the 'Fighting Fifth' and this is the name which stuck. The Duke of Wellington himself almost sighed about them: 'The Ever-fighting, Never-failing Fifth.'

Between 1674–1751 it took part in:

The Nine Years War, where ironically they spent 5 years fighting in Flanders;

---

37 If any readers can give any details about this extraordinary moment in Geordie history, please feel free to ring me at any hour of the day or night.

The War of Spanish Succession where they were one of four English regiments who fought a rearguard action with their Portuguese allies at Campo Maior in 1709, and also on the River Caia;

The Anglo- Spanish War where the regiment formed part of the garrison of Gibraltar which withstood the four-month long Spanish siege.

Then there was the **Seven Years War** in which the regiment took part in the Raid on Cherbourg in 1758, the Battle of Warburg in 1760, the Battle of Kirch Denkern in 1761 (where they captured the entire French Rouge regiment) and the Battle of Wilhelmsthal in 1762.

This is where they really made their name. At Wilhemstahl, in what is now North West Germany, they took more than twice their number of French grenadier prisoners and finally helped to capture nearly a whole French division.

Because of this exceptional feat the Fighting Fifth were for many years allowed to wear French grenadier caps, instead of the ordinary hat in use by the other British troops of the day. To show his admiration of their prowess Prince Ferdinand of Brunswick presented them with a snuff-box. I'm sure the front line Geordies, exhausted and bloodied after being stormed at with shot and shell in order to save his Prussian arse were very grateful for the snuff box, and tugged their forelocks appropriately.

Later, at the battle of St Lucie, the regiment was attacked by an army of 9000 very angry Frenchmen, but they were driven off with 500 killed and 1100 wounded; the Fighting Fifth lost 15 killed and 130 wounded. For this notable victory they were allowed to wear a red and white hackle feather in the head-dress, which was unique to the Northumberland Fusiliers. They wore it on ceremonial occasions and had a particularly big ceremony every St George's Day – which of course was St Geordie's Day.

They fought during in the American Revolution and won pretty much every large or small skirmish they were involved with. People spoke with admiration of their exceptional esprit de corps – and they hammered the French whenever they met them.

But it really earned its honours during the Peninsular War, when it formed part of a small force which beat off an overwhelming body of the enemy at El Boden on September 24th 1811. This was a performance which Wellington himself described as "a memorable example of what can be done by steadiness, discipline, and confidence." Northumbrians have never been short of confidence. At that time also they completely sealed their reputation as being either very brave men or complete nutters when the infantry charged the French cavalry with bayonets – and won the day.

The Marquis of Londonderry gave a stirring description of this affair. The French attack began, as he wrote, with a column of French cavalry charging the heights in gallant style, cheering in the usual manner of the French and making directly for the guns:

'The artillerymen stood their ground resolutely, giving their fare to the last; but there being nothing immediately at hand to support them, they were compelled to retire, and the guns fell for the moment into the hands of the assailants.'

But, when all seemed lost, someone gave the order to unleash the Geordies.

'They marched up in line, firing with great coolness, and when at a distance of only a few paces from their adversaries, brought their bayonets to the charging position and rushed forward. This is, I believe, the first instance on record of the charge of the bayonet being made upon cavalry by infantry in line; nor, perhaps, would it be prudent to introduce the practice. But never was a charge more successful. Possessing the advantage of ground, and keeping in close and compact array, the 5th literally pushed their adversaries down the hill, retook the guns, and limbering them to the horses, which had followed their advance, removed them safely.'[38]

The 5th (Northumberland Fusiliers) Regiment of Foot as it became known from 1881 also saw active service in the Indian Rebellion of 1857 where, at the siege of Arrah, they first used this new invention known as the Enfield rifle with its unique conical bullets, variations of which generations of Geordie soldiers would come to know very well indeed.

And the there was Second Anglo-Afghan War and the Boer War, followed by time spent suppressing riots in Belfast where, during the August and September of 1886, the detachment was called out to aid the civil authorities no fewer than twenty-five times.

During all these times which they did all the things that good soldiers should, and probably a lot of things that decent human beings shouldn't, but no-one who served in the Fighting Fifth was

---

[38] Quoted in *The Northumberland Fusiliers*, by Walter Wood. Published by G. Richards 1901.

unaware of its reputation as being a very tough regiment indeed. [39]

And by god they couldn't half tell some tales about it all to the new recruits. Especially the entirely true one about how the Kaiser was so worried about the Geordies that he bombed them in their tribal lands with his Zeppelins. When he did that, he became the best recruiter of them all.

It's often a complete surprise to learn that the civilian population of England was heavily bombed by the Germans during World War 1 as well World War 2. The Zeppelins conducted 43 raids, dropping 162 tons of bombs which killed 474 people and wounded 1146 others. Later, their far more efficient Gotha bombers made 27 raids, killing 835 and severely wounding 1,990 others and causing damage worth around £3,000,000. The main aim was entirely psychological. By appearing powerful in the skies above they sought to instil fear and panic in the populace below.

In the early years of the war the Kaiser refused to allow any Zeppelin or bomber raids on London. After all, the Kaiser and King George were cousins. So he ordered his nascent Luftwaffe to target the North East instead and try to damage any or all of those factories which were clagged along both banks of the Tyne.

The first attack on the North-East coast was aimed at Tynemouth on the night of April 14/15th 1915, but the crew of Zeppelin L9 mistook the Wansbeck for the Tyne and the bombs fell on Blyth.

Geordie could have watched the fires from the top window in the little tower on the Grand Hotel but he wouldn't have read too many details in the papers because censorship was such during the First World War that, for years afterwards, accounts of some of its most dramatic episodes could only be put together like pieces in a jigsaw puzzle.

Another, bigger attack was made in the early afternoon of 15th June, in calm weather conditions, when Zeppelins L10 and L11 piloted by Kapitänleutnant Hirsch and Oberleutnant Freiherr von Buttlar respectively, set off from Nordholz in northern Germany in

---

[39] During the Great War the Fusiliers would win numerous Battle Honours, were awarded 5 Victoria Crosses, and suffered 16,000 fatalities with probably four times that number wounded.

an almost direct line north-west. L11 broke its crankshaft after only an hour and returned home, but its sister dirigible carried on.

They both had enough ordnance on board to do a great deal of physical damage, quite apart from the poisons of Shock, Despondency and Awe they hoped to inject within the peoples. Their bombs came in 110, 128, 220 and 660 pound sizes. They also had large numbers of incendiary bombs, made of thermite wrapped in tarred rope, which weighed only 25 pounds but could devastate whole streets if used properly. The bombs were carried amidships, in racks on either side of the keel, and were released from a little silver switch on a board in the control car.

Captain Hirsch was aiming for the industrial heartlands of Newcastle but he was careful to avoid the coastal defences at Tynemouth, so approached via Blyth, some ten miles up the coast.

These defences seem simple enough today but they were cutting edge then, and involved parabolic sound mirrors angled slightly upwards. These Fulwell Mirrors as they were called consisted of a 15ft concave shape cut into a flat concrete wall, which had two smaller walls jutting out from it to stabilise the structure, and to exclude any noises which could interfere with the mirror's operation. Such mirrors reflected and amplified the noise of an aircraft's engines, so that a listener, situated in a trench shelter in front of the mirror, could raise the alarm.

By around 11 p.m. and flying at a height of 1,300 feet, the bold Kapitan wasn't too sure whether the river below him was the Wansbeck, the River Blyth, the Tyne itself or the River Wear, but there were no searchlights, no anti-aircraft fire, no fighter planes and all of the lights in the factories below were – as the Geordies would say – bleezin.

After bombing the Marine Engineering Works in Wallsend causing £30,000 worth of damage, he then bombed collieries both there and in Hebburn, though the lads underground wouldn't have heard a thing. From there he turned his attention to Palmer's shipyard at Jarrow, which was building the super-dreadnought battleship Resolution and two monitors for the Royal Navy. Here, seven of his high explosive and five incendiary bombs were dropped on the engine construction department, causing very severe damage and killing seventeen, injuring seventy-two others. On the way out he dropped bombs on Willington quay, East Howdon, Cookson's antimony works and Pochin's chemical works, then set the scenic railway ablaze near the Harton colliery staithes before making a stately exit via South Shields.

In all, 2.5 tonnes of high explosive and incendiary bombs were dropped and the effect was devastating. The glare of the bombing could be seen from 30 miles away.

Two of the largely useless FK3 fighter planes took off from Whitley Bay but the great silver cigar rose to over 5000 feet and they failed to climb fast enough. The Zeppelin's top speed of 84 miles an hour was just enough to elude them.

Then Whitley Bay, Jarrow, Wallsend and South Shields were attacked again on the night of 8/9 August 1916.

His Majesty's Government no longer needed to try and tease, torment or trick this lot of Geordies into battle by using propaganda about bayoneted babies or crucified nuns or tortured miners. Them Zeppelins gave the Geordies a very Big Push of their own...

6

THE NAMING OF THE PARTS

When he joined up, Geordie wasn't exactly a sacrificial lamb whose only role was to make up the numbers and go *baa* when prodded by the gentry. The man was a born survivor and you needed brains for that. You couldn't that say he was educated in the sense that his officers would have been, but letters have survived that he wrote to his second son William in 1943 which give a sort of sideways insight into his learning.[40]

Geordie had been notified that his son had been killed in action in Tobruk but the Red Cross found him in a Prisoner of War camp in Di Parma. Both father and son reckoned that the cowardly Italians were – as usual – doing the dirty work – as ever – of the Germans.

William had been very badly injured and had his legs blown off by a German 'daisy cutter', which was a bomb with an extension rod screwed into the nose to give it an air-burst, rather than just make a crater that soldiers can shelter in. If anyone knew about bombs and shells and German military perfidy it was William's dad, who had faced those German gas attacks which broke all the rules of war and seen the demonic use of their flame-throwers.

A series of slim letters were allowed to be exchanged between Wor Geordie and his son Bill, designated KRIEGSGEFANGENPOST which simply meant 'Prisoner of War Post'.

Bill's return letters to grandad haven't survived but it's clear from Geordie's replies where his son's main interest lay. The young man never mentioned his appalling wounds, or asked very much about his Mam or his siblings. He wasn't interested in the progress of the war and knew that anything about this would never get past the censor. He was in a stinking camp, in great pain, far from home and with very little hope – but he wanted as many details as his dad could provide about the football – especially the Newcastle v. Sunderland matches that had just started up again.

---

40 As I'll explain, these letters came courtesy of my cousin Bill, with thanks to the late Douglas Haig for making their appearance possible.

And Pop, as Wor Geordie signed himself, did his very best to provide.

He wrote carefully to his son, in full control of the language. In the small space allowed he answered all of Billy's questions. These letters, written on a delicate kind of oilskin, if that's the right term, show a greater level of fluency than the letters I have from my own Dad who had four more years of schooling. You can see in his replies that old soldier Geordie understands about the censorship that would be imposed both ways, and nicely judges what to write, cramming as much in as he can, giving Billy all the information he craved and needed, and adding almost as a postscript on one of them that his brother George had won £36 on Littlewoods Football Pools only a few weeks ago.

That waz a lot o' money then, son.
Was Mam pleased?
Ah didn't tell her.

It wasn't just luck that enabled him to survive three years on the Western Front. Geordie had a real brain under that tin helmet he would wear. The Elementary Education Act, which became law just two years before he was born, ensured that he had compulsory attendance at Elswick School from the age 5 to 10 years. He seems to have put that five years to good use.

The poorer families had problems with this Act and tried to send their children out to get whatever work they could, regardless of their age. So when Geordie was described on the Census returns of 1891 as a 'Scholar' this actually had a precise and necessary definition, intended to avoid any visit from the Attendance Officers who would visit homes and make sure the law was being upheld.

After the age of 10 and before they reached 13, any child employed was required to have an Educational Standard certificate to show they had reached a minimum standard of learning, else they and their families would be penalised.

Compared to some of the people in the area, the Richardsons of Rendel Street, Elswick would have been almost middle class. There were nine of them crammed into that small house: the parents Thomas and Sarah, and their children Margaret, Gilbert, Ada, our George, Thomas, William and Joseph. But there were also three incomes: Thomas was a Cranesman, Margaret was a stocking machinist and eldest son Gilbert, 15, was an Apprentice Blacksmith at Armstrong's Factory.

In contrast, Geordie's officers in the early years of the war were, without exception, highly educated individuals from public schools.[41] They would have sat in the trenches, in their officers' dugouts, tucking into their tins of Machonochie Stew, sighing with fond memories of their alma maters. Geordie, a married man who knew what went where and why, would have listened to them and looked back with fondness to the nearest thing he had ever had to an alma mater:

St George's Drill Hall.

The very name is more of a title than an actual address. Wherever the Northumberland Fusiliers meet and drill in peacetime becomes St George's. In 1914 it was situated in Northumberland Road, just a short walk along the Scotswood Road from his parents' house. He would have seen the young Saturday Soldiers coming and going while he was still a boy, and wanted some of that.

If you were to track down the same address today it will take you to the Anatomy Teaching Centre, Drill Hall, Northumberland Road where they teach you all sorts of Life Sciences, and their literature features pictures of enormously cheerful young souls who want to help, heal and improve the lot of their fellow men.

When Geordie went there, all he wanted to learn was how to blow the Germans to bits.

When our Geordie finally joined up he would have been given Army Form B.2512 – "Short Service, Attestation Of", known as his Attestation Papers. His have long since been burned into their constituent atoms but there is enough information now to fill in many of the gaps.

Corps & Regimental Number: 6th Battalion Noth'd Fus. TF. 4214
Date
Name & address: Richardson, G.M.
81 Castle Terrace, Hirst, Ashington

---

41 To my cousin in America: in England, 'public schools' here are actually private boarding schools.

THE NAMING OF THE PARTS

Nationality	English
Age	33
Trade	Barman
Marital status	Married
Previous military service	Territorial Force

If we can add a date in the blank space for purely mythopoetic reasons then it has to be St George's Day, April 23rd 1915.

With these details complete he would have raised his hand and taken an Oath of Allegiance in the presence of some dignitary, and I'd like to have seen that.

I've been in the presence of tough Northumbrian miners and their tougher wives who haven't shown the slightest interest when Queen Elizabeth the Queen Mother opened a park in Ashington, and whose parents wouldn't have crossed the back yard to look at Princess Alexandra when she visited. Yet the same types went all gooey in the presence of the Duke and Duchess of Northumberland as they strolled past in the pleasure gardens of Alnwick. They were *true* royalty.

It must be that tribal thing again. Since its third creation in 1766, the title 'Duke of Northumberland' has belonged to the House of Percy (Porsy), which held the title of Earl of Northumberland from 1377. The traditional burial place of the Dukes of Northumberland is Westminster Abbey in London, with the Percys being the last family to maintain such a privilege.

The House of Windsor, after all, only became such in 1917. Before that it was the House of Saxe-Coburg-Gotha. In the eyes of some (though not all) Geordies that lot doon in London were aall bliddy Jarmins. When Geordie took his oath it wasn't necessarily to King George as such, but to what lay beneath him – literally. Geordie took his oath to what he felt represented England. This was not the geo-political entity centred in Westminster with an Empire ruled by stiff-upper-lipped toffs with their fine wine, starched collars and cavalry charges. His England was one of the Cheviot Hills and moors, black-faced sheep, wild white cattle, pits and ponies and greyhounds, pubs and pints, endless beaches of golden sand and high dunes and a folk who never took themselves – or anyone else – too seriously. The King – with Jarmin blood or not – was just a symbol of all that which he'd be willing to die to protect. Especially the bairns.

Oaths are serious business though, and despite the inherent self-mocking, tongue-in-cheek nature of the Northumbrian native, he would have meant what he said insofar as it related to his land.

The oath went as follows:

> I, George Matthew Richardson, swear by Almighty God, that I will be faithful and bear true Allegiance to His Majesty King George the Fifth, His Heirs and Successors, and that I will, as in duty bound, honestly and faithfully defend His Majesty, His Heirs and Successors, In Person, Crown, and dignity against all enemies, and will observe and obey all orders of His Majesty, His Heirs and Successors, and of the Generals and Officers set over me. So help me God.

Once his words had stopped echoing in the large hall, and once the ink was dry on that contract, his life changed forever.

When war was declared, all Territorial Force troops received orders to mobilise. Even though many of them had just come back from the annual fortnight's training camp they were still hurriedly recalled to the home base. Most TF units had a pre-arranged war station and the various units were moved quickly to take up their designated places at these. Some were sent to garrison duties at various points around the Empire, replacing the regular units that were going to be called to serve in France.

As I said before, the Territorial Battalions were designed either as Front Line (1), Home (2), or Reserve (3), so the 6th Battalion of the Northumberland Fusiliers (TF) was broken down into groups:

1/6th Bn. Territorial Force. The prefix 1/ showed that this section of the 6th Battalion was for Front Line or Overseas duty. The men who chose this were all volunteers. They were soon part of the Northumbrian Division (50th Div. as it was written).

Those who did not want to fight overseas but who would willingly give their lives to defend their nation on their own home soil were placed in what was given as 2/6th Bn. Territorial Force. This lot joined the 188th Brigade, 63rd Division and were promptly sent overseas anyway, and made some of the lads feel they'd been lied to and cheated. Yet by that time the situation at the Front was

THE NAMING OF THE PARTS

so serious that King George needed every trained Geordie he could get.

The 3/6th Bn. Territorial Force, then, was formed to train up recruits that would eventually join the 1/6th Bn. I'll talk about the numerous other Battalions later.

So now we've got our Geordie avatar signed up, with his Oath still echoing up through a huge hall which reeked with subtle undertones of disinfectant, boot polish, gun oil, cigarettes and Brasso. But apart from the cheerful, slightly cheeky but also rather shy face that we can use from his photograph, what was he like physically?

⚙

The British soldier in 1914 had to be at least 5' 3" tall, although this minimum requirement was gradually lowered as the slaughter increased, until eventually a few Bantam Battalions were formed which the Germans thought were hilarious. Those were tough little bastards though, many of them ex-miners, and their Mills bombs would kill just as well as the next.

There was only about two inches difference in average height between 21-year-old males in 1912 and 2012 (5' 8" and 5' 10" respectively) so Geordie could pass in a modern crowd and we wouldn't notice. My Dad and his brothers were all handsome, strapping six-footers and proud of the fact. I was six foot when I was 16 and looked like one of the matchstick men from L.S. Lowry's paintings and hated myself.

As I write this I have a clear, possibly irrelevant (but genuine) memory of something from around the year 1967 which won't go away, and so I must include it.

In some ways the events in question were a microcosm of all those national tensions that caused people to kill each other in the Great War, and probably hint at the causes of dysfunction within families too.

Quite simply the football team from my school, Ashington County Grammar, played that of the Hirst East Secondary Modern in Portland Park in an end of season life-or-death competition. This is the park where Geordie would have gone to watch local matches, or place bets on the greyhounds. The pupils of both schools were on opposite sides of the pitch, in the noisy wooden stands, and there was no fraternising with the enemy.

We were in our blue and grey uniforms with stripey ties, they in their street clothes. I know they saw us as I saw that young officer in my dreams: delicate, stuck-up softies with arrogant attitude but no substance – a baseless sense of superiority. We saw them as inferior, crass thickos who were always spoiling for a fight.

Their behaviour toward us was scarcely human: some of the hand gestures they made in our direction were… well, rather shocking. As the eye scanned along the two teams lined up before kick-off I noticed there was a very marked difference in height. In fact us grammar school 'snerbs', as they called us, were – all of us – about a foot taller than the Eastie yobs, as we called them.[42]

Yet we were all from the same background. Our fathers all worked in the same pits. We all had the same diet and the disadvantages.

This is something which has bothered me all my life, and I suppose will never be explained. We were all nascent Tory-loathing socialists, every schoolboy there, but with no sense of kinship across the barrier of the pitch and the mutual loathing broiled between us like poison gas. The Fusiliers at Thiepval and the Germans which faced them probably felt a greater sense of soldierly understanding and amity than the opposing pupils that day.

We demonised each other. We saw – or imagined we saw – the evils we went looking for. We spun yarns about each others' foibles and failings, although I suspect their perceptions of us had some degree of truth in them. The war on that pitch was inevitable. And had they charged us across the field, I would have run a mile because they could have torn us apart.

So when I read about the Bantam Battalions and their lack of height being caused purely by deficient social factors I think of that time when two lots of 'scholars' faced each other at Portland Park, and recall how the Eastie Lads (and my Dad, who never knew what to make of me, had been one) would have machine-gunned the lot of us.[43]

Yet we were also – tall or small – what we would now call ectomorphs.

Eh?

Like greyhounds Dad. Thin as rakes, but wiry and very strong.

---

42 To translate: snerb = snob.
43 PS we stuffed the little gits 3-2. Both their goals were miles offside.

Ye could nivver beat iz at arm wrasslin though. Ye needed real *muscles for that.*

Bulk or not, I suppose I want to create Geordie in my own image by making him about 5' 10", slim but not scrawny and without the long, slightly bandy hairy legs which have been the curse of some Richardsons down through the aeons.

In creating this avatar in order to experience something of what Geordie or any new recruit felt in the Great War, we have to clothe him. If we can get a sense of what someone might have been like just by handling something he once owned, like the watch, it's possible to get something of the same effect by assuming his form, starting on the outside and working in. For a man it's easy to do this: in your mind's eye clothe yourself in the British Army uniform of the time. Feel the weight, the cut, the starch in the shirts, the texture of the fabrics. For a woman, imagine what the young man felt like, fully kitted out, proud as Lucifer and seeking your admiration.

So we have to learn what his uniform looked like, what it felt like to wear and try to put ourselves – almost literally – in his boots. We have to imagine that we've been quite shoddily dressed all our lives and now find ourselves in the sort of uniform that would attract glances everywhere, making us feel the equal of everyone.

If you enter the Great War at different periods you will get different stories. After conscription was brought into force the tales are inevitably of the anxious new recruits being given ill-fitting bits of uniforms, which they had to swap with those around them until they got an outfit that almost fitted. But this was not due to government indifference so much as the huge surge of new soldiers outstripping the supplies.

I'm assuming that Geordie got in slightly before the rest so that for the first time in his life he got into clothes that, while not quite made-to-measure, fitted him rather well. He might not have looked like *The Man Who Broke the Bank at Monte Carlo*, as the musical hall song went, but he would have felt pretty damned good.

In fact the British Army of 1914 was never seen as rag-bags except by themselves. It was the best trained, best equipped and best organised soldiery that we had ever sent to war. Both German and American assessments agreed that our equipment was of the highest order. Henry T. Allen commented: 'As to horses, equipment and wagons, the British are easily ahead of any troops of the allies.'[44]

The French wore highly visible blue coats and red trousers, and sometimes their kit included reflective ceremonial breastplates which had no practical purpose on the battlefield. They may have fought with sartorial flair but it took them some months to realise that they were all bullet magnets.

The outfit that Geordie pulled on was smart, practical, and looked a lot better than the bad-fitting grey, convict-like uniforms of the Jarmins. The new khaki of the British soldier was, according to some, the colour of shite; in some areas of Flanders it would be the colour mud. As the world's first attempt at camouflage in a uniform, Geordie's kit was years ahead of its time. When young boys in Britain in the 1980s watched the SAS on telly storming the Iranian Embassy in that black clobber which made them look like Angels of Death, large numbers of them decided they wanted some of that. Geordie's own uniform would have had a similar effect on the youngsters who saw him strutting along the avenues in Ashington.

In fact in 1914, before the severity of the conflict began to filter back home, there was a charming piece of doggerel which went:

When a call to arms was answered by a hundred thousand men
There were lots of chaps in Britain, 'twixt the age of four and ten
Who'd have answered to their country's call and hurried off to war
If Kitchener had but reduced the fighting age to four.

Whoever penned that was stupid, smug and should have been put up against the wall and shot, like that Billy Kinghorn of Whitley Bay. But she was also right. Those kids in the backstreets would have shown Geordie respect as a soldier that he would never have got as mere barman.

In fact, 40 years after he joined up the most popular game boys aged 4-10 played in Ashington was 'Japs and English', though god knows why. I'm not sure if the Northumberland Fusiliers ever fought out there in World War 2 and passed the stories down to us. But the call to arms, even though our guns were either imaginary, wooden sticks, or new-fangled plastic, was irresistible. Believe me I

---

44 *My Rhineland Journey*, London 1924

was out there with the rest of them, even though I was always made to be one of the Japs, shouting *Banzai Bonny Lads!* as I charged the cunningly concealed machine gun nest which was pouring withering fire – and a lot spittle – from the coalhouse next door.

If he'd been alive then, I can't imagine that Grandad would have smiled approvingly.

If we have to start looking at our avatar's clothing properly, we must risk getting our pixels dirty and start with the underwear.

In 1900 poor women made theirs from old bags that grocers had kept rice or flour in. Their men and their children often didn't wear anything.

In those days before central heating, if you had a job and thus a bit of spare cash, the discerning male would wear what we would now think of as 'long johns', also known as union suits. This was a one-piece, knitted undergarment that covered the body from the ankles to the wrists. It had a long row of buttons up the front and featured a buttoned drop seat in the rear. You can see these in co'boy fillums all the time, and my maternal grandfather, Henry Tarbit, never seemed to take his off. However these often shrunk when washed, making them uncomfortable to wear – especially when Geordie had to do a long shift at the Grand Hotel.

The Territorials, however, issued him with two pairs of very soft woollen underpants, of the sort that posh folk called drawers. When he pulled a pair of these on for the first time he felt it was worth joining up for these alone. Plus he would have had some fun showing them off to Jinny: *Howay pet, hev a feel o' these. See if ye can get these buttons tae work. Ooh! Oh aye, that's nice...* That's probably when little May was conceived. And these kecks weren't the sort of self-destructing rubbish his descendants would get from Arrowsmiths corner shop a generation later: these ones weighed over a pound, and that was before they got wet, sweaty and started to turn yellow at the front. They were allowed to change them once a month for a fresh pair.

So bliddy middle class, eh?
Aye Dad, ideas above his station.

He would have had fun with the rival Tyneside Scottish battalions, largely recruited from Geordies who lived along the river in Wallsend. Although only about 20% of them were actually from Scotland, their commander, out of sheer affectation, had them issued with kilts as if they were a real Highland regiment. No underpants for them. 'Harder than Hammers' was their motto. Quite apart from the sheer impracticality of the kilt when it came to trench life in winter, this caused serious problems during the gas attacks because of the effect that chlorine (or other chemicals) would have upon the naked skin. The Tyneside Scottish were then issued a type of tough canvas underpants that the troops called trench bloomers. They tied off, just above the knee to stop the effects of gas on crucial areas but their lower limbs suffered. Eventually the Tyneside Scottish battalions were absorbed into the Northumberland Fusiliers and wore the same uniform as Geordie, much to the delight of their bollocks if not their Lieutenant Colonel.

Then came the socks. Three pairs of them. These would be as important as the Enfield rifle he was aching to get ahold of. New recruits were shown photographs of the deformations caused by trench foot. These were as horrifying as the images they would also be shown of the syphilis they would surely catch if they cavorted with the dorty wimmen in France. If the foot turned gangrenous, as it invariably did, then after appalling agony you would lose a whole leg. The only remedy for trench foot was for the soldiers to dry their feet and change their socks several times a day. This was not a luxury, it was compulsory. As well as this, soldiers were told to cover their feet with a special grease made from whale-oil. Each battalion at the front would use ten gallons of the stuff every day.

Socks were recognised as so important to the war effort that millions of women on all fronts knitted furiously, sending socks and various other kinds of foot comforters to their menfolk.

The hat. You had to have a hat. There was something very odd about a man who didn't wear one. You could often tell class and status as much by what was on the head as by the words which came from the mouth. All men wore hats in those days. Until he was an old man and realised that no-one bothered about such things any more, my Dad would wear his cloth cap just to go to the corner shop.

Wor Geordie's first military cap would have been what they called the Gor Blimey, or Trench Cap, which had a stiffened peak (from which they soon removed the wire) and flaps which could pull down to cover the ears in winter. Later this was replaced by a much softer version which could be folded up into a pocket when wearing the steel helmet. (These were both far more practical and comfortable than the later Universal Pattern Field Service Cap, which was used throughout World War II when the helmet wasn't being worn. They may have been stylish, and favoured by royalty, but they were known to the squaddies – not affectionately – as Cunt Caps.)

And this Trench Cap was supplemented by the all-important iconic 'tin hat' which looks incredibly old-fashioned to us now but which made eyes water with their innovatory brilliance in 1915.

The first of the tin hats were made of thick steel which could be formed from a single pressing – and thus churned out cheaply and quickly. These were soon modified into the Type B version which used a harder steel with 12% manganese content. This one had a narrower brim and a more domed crown and could withstand a .45 calibre pistol bullet travelling at 600 feet per second fired at a distance of 10 feet. It was far tougher than the German equivalent and saved countless lives. It would also serve as a piss-pot or for crapping in when necessary, and there was nothing too primitive about that. Until the National Coal Board was shamed into modernising the miners' houses in Ashington around the year 1968 we all had outdoor toilets and enamel piss-pots under the bed whether we went to the grammar school or not.

※

The tunic. Geordie's new thick woollen tunic, dyed khaki, had two breast pockets for personal items and his very important AB64 Pay Book: he wasn't going to war for nothing. There were also two smaller pockets for other things, and an internal pocket sewn under the right flap of the lower tunic where the First Field Dressing was kept.

Special patches known as rifle patches were sewn above the breast pockets, to prevent wear from the webbing equipment and rifle. Shoulder straps were sewn on and fastened with brass buttons, with enough space for a brass regimental shoulder title. Rank insignia was sewn onto the upper tunic sleeves.

Later they would be issued with buttons which changed colour in the presence of gas.

The trousers were made from khaki serge wool. The waistband had 14 buttons for the braces and was lined with white cotton.

Then came the puttees which were a flamin' nuisance to put on but kept the legs warm and the trench rats from shooting up your trouser legs. This is not a joke. A puttee (from the Hindi word, *pattah*, meaning 'strip of cloth') was wrapped from the ground up, and the top of each was tied with cotton tape. Traditional military puttees were made from khaki broadcloth, typically dyed to match the colour of the wearer's uniform, although wool was sometimes used also.

And then came the boots. It should be possible to tell the entire history of the British Army in terms of its boots alone. There has never been a conflict in which it has stomped into battle and been completely happy with its footgear. These were known as ammunition boots, which were unlined ankle-boots with leather laces, iron heel-plate and toe-plate, and an iron-studded leather sole. They were designed to be hard-wearing and long-lasting rather than comfortable. The hobnailed soles made a loud sound when the wearer was marching and some wags nicknamed them 'crunchies', but Geordie found that if you scuffed your feet on the pavement as you walked along you could make sparks fly in the night and everybody would get oot the way. When Germans killed Tommies one of the first things they did was remove what they saw as their excellent boots.

Are ye mekkin' this aall up son? Or ye being mytho-bliddy-poetic agayn?

I tried your tackety pit-boots on once which were just the same as Army boots an' I made sparks up and doon the backyard.
An Ah bet yer Mam thowt ye were wonderful.
She did actually. I could do no wrong, could I?
An' Ah couldn't dae a single thing right...

When I joined the Air Training Corps in the mid 1960s we were issued with boots that were not dissimilar to the ones Geordie had been given – and we got the same immutable advice that had been passed down through the generations like an 11th Commandment: Thou shalt piss in thy boots before you try to walk in them.[45]

There were two ways that we could soften the leather. Officers could pour some whisky into them and leave them for a couple of nights. Other ranks could piss in them, ditto. The latter method was known as the 'sweet pea' remedy.

As if this was not enough Geordie was then fitted with the complex webbing equipment which finally laced him into his destiny.

The 1908 Pattern Webbing equipment consisted of: a wide belt, left and right ammunition pouches which held 75 rounds each; left and right braces; a small sheath known as a 'frog' for the bayonet; an attachment for the entrenching tool handle; an entrenching tool head in web cover; a carrier for the blue-enamelled steel water bottle which was covered with khaki cloth; small haversack and large pack. Also, when they marched into combat during the war's later years the soldiers were given an extra ammunition bandolier: a simple cotton container with five pockets each holding two five-round clips. This webbing equipment was a big advance in design on anything that had gone before, as it placed no restriction on the chest and could be removed in one piece if necessary, by unfastening the belt.

Then he had his mess tin which was worn attached to one of the packs, and contained inside a cloth buff-coloured khaki cover.

Inside the haversack were personal items, shaving gear, two days rations of corned beef and biscuits, a knife, and when on Active

---

[45] Most of us in that intake of the ATC were from the grammar school. The Eastie lads joined the Army Cadet Force. We all got the same advice about our boots.

Service, unused portions of the daily ration which Geordies call 'bait'. The large pack could sometimes be used to house some of these items, but was normally kept for carrying the soldier's heavy greatcoat and/or a waterproof groundsheet.

His rifle, bayonet and ammunition alone weighed 20 lbs, and by the time he was fully kitted out and proud as hell, Geordie would be carrying over 70 lbs of clothing, weapons and equipment. This would be even heavier if he carried one of the specialist weapons we'll look at later. And that doesn't include the gas mask.

Of course, officers had their Soldier Servants to do most of their carrying and didn't have all this webbing to worry about. And when the men marched to battle, officers rode alongside them on horseback. Their burdens were all to do with leadership on the field. Christopher Duffy's superb book *Through German Eyes*, drawing on German intelligence assessments made throughout the Great War, reveals that the British commanders were often scornfully known as 'golfing officers': deemed to be devoid of experience, with no idea of the wider picture but sometimes brave to the point of rashness – if only to conceal how ignorant they were.

I don't think Geordie would have disagreed too much with that assessment.

So Geordie's Territorials were not a rag-bag army thrown into the fray just to make up the numbers. At best, they were very well-equipped indeed. By this time I'd also come to glimpse something of the astonishing, meticulously planned and absolutely first-rate build-up to that dire date of July 1st, such that if I'd been alongside Geordie that day, I'd have been quietly confident that nothing could possibly go wrong, having seen the preparations made for the well-being of every soldier there.

Grandad's war, like troubled family relationships glimpsed from afar, was proving to be not quite as black and white as I'd first thought. Sure, some of the Fusiliers' officers might have been more at home with their Mashie Niblicks on the 18th Hole, but some of them led from the front and inspired their men to run with them through brick walls or – even worse – into the chest-deep mud of No Man's Land. Certainly our tactics might have seemed (and certainly been) inept at times to the point of idiocy, but often from the German point of view they were devastatingly effective.

Even the enemy's assessments of the Territorials' capabilities conceded that by February 1916 the TF divisions were almost matching the efficiency of the Regular Army. From a German Intelligence report of the time:

> The [Territorial] men make a favourable military impression, and are physically remarkably fresh. Most of them are still young...and they are not as rigid in their bearing as some of the men from the Kitchener battalions, where the discipline is anyway much more strict. The men from any given battalion hail from the same locality and are mostly friends...[46]

The well-known writer and radio broadcaster J.B. Priestley had, as a young man, served in the 10th Battalion, the Duke of Wellington's Regiment, in which he was he was wounded in 1916 by mortar fire. Although in his autobiography *Margin Released* he is fiercely critical of the British Army, and in particular the officer class, his comments about the training he received would be just as relevant to the Territorial Battalions:

> It is not true, as some critics of the First War British high command have suggested, that Kitchener's army consisted of brave but half-trained amateurs, so much pitiful cannon-fodder. In the earlier divisions like ours, the troops had months and months of severe intensive training. Our average programme was ten hours a day, and nobody grumbled more than the old regulars who had never been compelled before to do so much and for so long.[47]

Here we are then, with our avatar fully clothed from feet up through bollocks to the top of his head and aching for only one last thing to make him complete: the superb Lee Enfield rifle. He would get that when he had been properly trained. He wasn't going to be allowed to wander the streets of Ashington with a thing like that, no matter how much he might need it when the pubs closed.

---

46 Christopher Duffy. *Through German Eyes* p70. Phoenix 2006
47 from: *Margin Released*, J. B. Priestley

7

GETTING STUCK IN

THE WATCH came back to me, fixed. As a matter of duty to my Dad I opened the rear case to check on the jewels: I had counted them all out and now I counted them all back: 17, glistening away, a nebula of stars. The dial was straight and secure, the glass was clear. They had polished the case so it gleamed. The new mainspring was now turning the arbor. All those greater and lesser gears which represent Geordie's family and which do things I don't fully understand, were turning as they should. For the first time in almost a century it made the noise it was meant to: tick tock tick tick...

Thank ye son. Thank ye very much.

Sitting close to the window to catch the morning light, I looked into the polished gold curves of the case, scrying as The Mam had done all those years ago, though I had none of the might-have-beens or should-have-beens that so damaged her own inner workings. I saw my face in there, curved out of shape, quizzical but hopeful. Startled, I looked like grandad but blurred, as through a prejudice darkly.

If I had, for many years, that totally false image of the young officer at dawn waiting to go over the top, I came to realise that I've done exactly the same with Private G.M. Richardson. If I've looked at and frequently judged the officer through ignorance and upbringing, I've done no less an injustice to Geordie too.

All my life I'd seen him in frozen tableaux: an old man in an antique war; an obsolete barman in a crumbling pub; an ancient wreck dying in his bed a whole aeon before I was born. Yet as I peered at my reflection in the watch and saw a fuzzy version of his own face peering through at me, I realised that when he died of cancer, in agony, he was younger than I am as I write this.

Now I'd really have to stop seeing the newly-recruited Fusiliers in that little cinema screen before my brow as Dad's Army types, old men creaking and groaning over laughable assault courses more appropriate to a modern playground. I had to straighten the curved vision of the past and see them all as young men of vigour and hope and realise that the training Geordie undertook was no less rigorous than anything offered by the Army today, but without the luxuries that modern soldiers have.

There is something about this idea of preparing for any sort of battle that can get the senses going. Whether it's Rocky turning himself from a shambling, breathless wreck into a man who could do one-handed push-ups and then bound up those steps in Philadelphia ready to take on Apollo Creed – or our own and very real Andy MacNab pushing himself through Selection process for the SAS on his way to his destiny with Brave Two Zero.

All those books about the Special Forces sell in huge quantities because the details of the training has the (male) reader gasping, following the character but making it his own, prompting every man and perhaps Everyman, to wonder if they too could have passed Selection or else done the same things but with flippers on for the rival Special Boat Service.

It's one of the appeals of all those games in which a whole generation sits on a couch before a large screen, and their idea of a Big Push involves mortal kombat using their thumbs, fulfilling their need for derring-do through those avatars that crash and thrash and blast their way through endless levels of cyber-spatial nothingness. Sometimes I think this almost mocks the real mortal combat that the Tommies went through in order to make these freedoms possible for us, though I wouldn't want my children to go anywhere near a real battlefield.

As for those young men and women today who sign up to fight in real but bewildering wars that never seem to end, in foreign climes where we don't even seem to be wanted, be assured that I've got the whole regiment of the Northumberland Fusiliers lined up in my psyche saluting every one of them.

Wor Geordie of flesh, blood and newly-issued uniform still had some way to go before he was issued with his rifle. He had to undergo a level of training that was aimed at making a new man of him, while learning along the way that this new world he found himself in was not always logical or fair, and that No Man's Land never is.

If we are to energise our own literary avatar of Geordie and build up his muscles, we need to look more closely at his training. Though before we do that we need to understand how Geordie as an individual fitted into the bewildering corporate mass, the sim city, that was the British Army in 1915. If you've ever wondered what exactly constituted a platoon, battalion, regiment and the rest, we can have a quick look now.

Let's start at the bottom and work upward.

The basic unit was the:

Section. This contained a corporal, with a lance corporal as second-in-command and six privates. Geordie never rose above Section level. Despite winning the medals that many of his most senior officers never achieved he entered the army as a private and left it at the same rank. We'll come back to that point later. Three sections of these eight men would constitute the:

Platoon. This would be commanded by a lieutenant or second lieutenant. In battle an NCO would assume command if the officer was killed. Four of these platoons would constitute a:

Company. This notionally comprised six officers, the most senior of whom would be major or captain. Companies were usually designated A,B,C, or D. There were varying numbers of Companies in the next cluster known as the:

Battalion. This was the principal fighting unit of the British Army during the Great War. Battalions were commanded by their Lieutenant Colonel who was assisted by twenty-nine officers. In theory each battalion would have just over 1000 officers and men, but in reality they often went into battle with far less than that. They also took into battle the wagons and carts needed to carry ammunition and supplies and some of the heavier weapons that Geordie would learn to use like the Vickers machine gun.

GETTING STUCK IN

Although looking at lists of Battalions can be as tedious as other peoples' genealogies, we can give them anyway for those whose relatives might have been involved. Apart from the first eight battalions of Northumberland Fusiliers we mentioned earlier there were also:

9th (Northumberland Hussars Yeomanry)	28th (Reserve) Battalion
10th & 11th Battalions	29th (Reserve) (Tyneside Scottish)
12th & 13th Battalions	30th (Reserve) (Tyneside Irish)
14th Battalion	31st (Reserve) Battalion
15th Battalion	33rd (Reserve) (Tyneside Scottish)
16th & 17th Battalions	34th (Reserve) (Tyneside Irish)
18th Battalion	35th Battalion
19th Battalion	36th Battalion
20th, 21st, 22nd & 23rd Tyneside Scottish	37th (Home Service) Battalion
24th, 25th, 26th & 27th Tyneside Irish	38th Battalion
	1st (Garrison) Battalion
	2nd (Garrison) Battalion
	3rd (Home Service) (Garrison)

The battalions then formed part of this almost mystical entity known as the:

Regiment. This is the body to which all soldiers felt their primary loyalty, led by a god-like Colonel. Unlike other nations, the British regiments never fought as one unified body. You would never have seen all the Geordie battalions in action at the same place at the same time. A number of them would have plucked out to form a:

Brigade. Brigades originally consisted of four battalions, but as the butchery increased this was sometimes reduced to three. The same thing happened to the battalions themselves, so that our Geordie's 6th Bn. seems to have taken such heavy casualties that it was melded into the 4th. If you were to follow the history of the 6t^h Bn. then you need to look up the events of the 4th, because they became one and the same. Above the Brigade came the:

Division. This contained three brigades of fighting soldiers but also all the extra support units it might need to fight as a miniature army: signallers, medics, engineers, gunners and transport. Like battalions, whole divisions were often moved during the war. And each division came under the command of the:

Corps. Each corps consisted of two or more divisions, and was led by a lieutenant-general. They used Roman numerals to identify themselves. This in turn was part of the:

Army. Each army was a fully-trained, combat-ready body of men commanded by a general. Each army consisted of two or more corps and all the other supporting units deemed necessary to wage effective war. At the start of the war there were two armies in France. By the end of the war, thanks to the massive numbers that volunteered for the New Armies, there were five.

Geordie's **Northumbrian Division** commanded by Major General B. Burton comprised in total:

Northumberland Brigade	York and Durham Brigade	Durham Light Infantry Brigade
Brigadier General J.F. Riddell	Brigadier General J.E. Bush	Brigadier General J.W. Sears
4th Bn Northumberland Fusiliers A Coy. B Coy. C Coy. D Coy.	4th Bn East Yorks Regiment A Coy. B Coy. C Coy. D Coy.	6th Bn Durham Light Infantry A Coy. B Coy. C Coy. D Coy.
5th Bn Northumberland Fusiliers A Coy. B Coy. C Coy. D Coy.	4th Bn Princess of Wales' Own A Coy. B Coy. C Coy. D Coy.	7th Bn Durham Light Infantry A Coy. B Coy. C Coy. D Coy.
6th Bn Northumberland Fusiliers A Coy. B Coy. C Coy. D Coy.	5th Bn Princess of Wales' Own A Coy. B Coy. C Coy. D Coy.	8th Bn Durham Light Infantry A Coy. B Coy. C Coy. D Coy.
7th Bn Northumberland Fusiliers A Coy. B Coy. C Coy. D Coy.	5th Bn Durham Light Infantry A Coy. B Coy. C Coy. D Coy.	9th Bn Durham Light Infantry A Coy. B Coy. C Coy. D Coy.

But the ability to draw men toward war and then keep them on the battlefield when they saw its full horrors was due in no small part to the power of the Regiment. When Geordie and his like went over the top – and kept going over the top – they did so not for King and Country and certainly not for any thoughts of liberating poor little Belgium: they did so for their mates. It has been the same in every regiment of the British Army in every field of battle since the system began.

Where did Private Richardson go for his actual training?

Many of the newer NF battalions were sent to Halton Park, near Tring, which was the French chateau-style stately home of

Alfred de Rothschild that had been turned over for military use. Old photographs show the grounds as being a vast tent city, and the French theme would have been homaged even more by training trenches that covered large parts of the once immaculate grounds.

But the Regiment, as we have seen, was never kept completely together. Records show that the 1/4th Battalion Northumberland Fusiliers, a territorial battalion, was based in Hexham when war broke out in August 1914. After nine months' training they proceeded to France in April 1915, to join the 149th Brigade, 50th (Northumbrian) Division. They were well documented.

The 5th Battalion had a famous memorial made of them called 'The Response'. This commemorated the time when they marched from their camp in Gosforth Park, through Haymarket, and on to Central Station before embarking to fight on the Western Front, watched by a soaring angel while women and children bade them farewell. Their grand Moment was preserved in stone for all time at Barras Bridge.[48]

But the 6th and 13th Bns to which Geordie belonged have proved as elusive as the man himself. They kept almost no records and their War Diary was fragmentary. This is probably because they were like two globs of quicksilver which got smashed into a million micro-globules by the German hammer.

There were a dozen training camps set up all over Northumberland and Durham. He would have been equally placed to go twenty miles north to Alnwick as to Fenham Barracks, in the heart of Newcastle. But because the Fusiliers gave me one of their 3 o'clock in the morning wake-up calls and sent me scurrying to the computer to start googling, I'm going to plump for Boldon Camp because that one came up as if by magic. It's not a perfect answer, because I also found a broken thread which said that the 6th Bn. had been billeted in houses scattered throughout Whitley Bay, Seaton Sluice, Seaton Delaval, Blyth, North Shields (all of which had been overflown by the Zeppelin), and these are all on the other side of the Tyne. Nothing survives of this particular training camp, and no-one from the excellent Boldon website[49] replies to my on-line queries. But I'll create our Virtual site here and call it 'Boldon' just to get started.

---

[48] The memorial bears the inscription "Non Sibi Sed Patriae" (Not for Self but for Country).

[49] http://www.boldononline.co.uk/

I found, however, an old grainy photograph from *The War Illustrated* 17th July 1915, taken at Boldon Camp, captioned: 'The art of the fighting man'. It shows three officers and six other ranks (including drummer and bugler) looking at the Honours List of the Northumberland Fusiliers as worked out in stone and flowers in a large bed, no doubt for the inspiration of the new recruits. The caption adds: 'The proud achievements of the Fusiliers from Wilhemstahl to Modder River are duly recorded. There will no doubt be fresh names added when the Huns are beaten.'

There certainly were. If you were to create in stone and flowers the whole Honours List for the NF during the Great War you would need a football field. As it is, I've put these in the Appendices to save space here.

If you were to google Boldon Camp yourself you will be taken to a vast variety of camping and caravan sites, learn lots about Boy Scouts, get various blurbs offering free lubes from Halfords (which I assume is something to do with bicycles) and get taken to one even more grainy photo of what seems to be disconsolate German Prisoners of World War 1 being marched somewhere. At the same time I got constant pop-ups from semi-naked Russian ladies who kept saying 'Hey Big Boy, I really like your profile and would love to talk.'

While I'm pleased that many young women in St Petersburg are now taking a healthy interest in the Northumberland Fusiliers, as a worrisome father of four girls I do wish they'd put on cardigans during this cold weather. Though why they should all be lurking in the cyber-space around East Boldon is something that my generation will probably never understand. Still, I'm sure I'll have some meaningful dialogue with them in due course, and would love to know their opinions about the triple-trench system used by the British Army at the Ypres Salient.

Can ye not just show some courtesy and reply to the lassies Alan?
Dad, they're not what they seem. They're hairy-arsed fellas named Boris.
An' Ah'm sure they speak very highly of you as well.

Recently archaeologists in search of prehistoric settlements on the brow of Hylton Castle, near East Boldon, stumbled upon what they marvelled at as World War 1 entrenchments, as if these were as antiquated as the stone adzes that inspired them. That strata of Geordie's life has been wiped from the world almost as much as his own personal history, but the rifle ranges in adjoining Whitburn can still be seen and are, apparently, still being used. This is where we can give Geordie his gun.

This gun would become as close to him as his wife, and the old soldiers all referred to their rifle as 'she'. As musketry instructors have always said in all the wars: 'Treat her right, and she'll give you full satisfaction.'

In fact he would probably treat it a lot better than he sometimes did Jinny. There was a pullthrough and oil bottle in the rifle's butt trap that he would have to use regularly; and he might have to boil the barrel out after a heavy firing but that was all part of the romance – and a lot more relaxed than the jig-a-jig of the marital bed. He would oil her, polish her, clean her inside and out and she would never get in a bad fettle like his lass. He would know her so intimately that he could tell from minute variations in weight whether there were rounds in the magazine or not. He would go to sleep cuddling her and still find her there the next day. There would never be a cross word and almost total empathy. He would clutch her lovingly and often with desperation. He would think her the most beautiful thing he'd ever seen. He would kill with her.

This was the legendary Short Magazine Lee Enfield Rifle, or the SMLE.

As something of a Beta Male even I can fully understand this. It is not about wanting to kill, but more to do with the beauty of the engineering and craftsmanship. Some twenty years ago I had a powerful air rifle. My then mother-in-law, who lived directly opposite in our narrow street, wanted me to shoot the huge crow that was bouncing on her telly aerial and making her screen all fuzzy. I couldn't. I could shoot at pictures of Kenny Dalglish at the bottom of the garden and take out his irises at 30 yards with a .22 lead slug, but the crow was always gonna be safe. Decades before this, when I fired real live Lee Enfields at an Air Training Corp camp and got my Marksman's Badge, it gave me more pride in being able to put five bullets into that small area of the target than many of my accomplishments since. Think what Geordie would have felt in those early days before he used it for real. To him, it would have been like holding Excalibur.

Could ye hev killed with it though?
To protect my family? Just give me another magazine and a full bandoleer, plus maybe three Mills bombs, a trench mortar and a Lewis Gun – and stand aside...
So you're a Geordie efter aall.
I'm a Dad, Dad.

The Fusiliers had first become familiar with the Enfield rifle at the siege of Arrah in 1857, and were quite taken with the increased range and accuracy of those new 'conical' bullets. That version went through constant development so that by the time Geordie was given the SMLE it had already evolved into a weapon that couldn't really be improved upon. It would still be the rifle of choice for the British Army for another forty years.

When George MacDonald Fraser was using his to good effect for the Cumbrian Border Regiment in the Burma Campaign of World War 2, he almost drooled over it as the most beautiful firearm ever invented.

> "I'm no Davy Crockett, but I could hit three falling plates (about ten inches square) out of five at two hundred [yards] and I was graded only a first-class shot, not a marksman. The Lee Enfield, cased in wood from butt to muzzle, could stand up to any rough treatment and it never jammed."[50]

It weighed just 8lb 10oz, had a barrel length of 25 inches and was 44 inches long in total.[51] It had a ten round box magazine that would be removed and manually loaded with the .303 British cartridges from the top, or by means of five-round chargers. Its muzzle velocity was 2,441 feet per second, with a maximum range of 3,000 yards, although if you tilted the gun upwards at an angle of 35 degrees you could get the bullet to travel 4,400 yards over a time of 30 seconds. Despite being sighted to 2000 yards, in reality its most effective distance was just under 600 – when you could get a clear look at

---

50 George MacDonald Fraser. *Quartered Safe Out Here*. p29. HarperCollins 2000
51 The Bantam Battalions had their stocks specially cut down so they could get them to their shoulders.

what was actually coming toward you. I make no apologies for not knowing what any of these distances are in modern litres.

This was quite simply the fastest military rifle of the day, and its downturned bolt was easier and quicker to manipulate than the straight versions of its rivals. The world record for aimed bolt-action fire was set in 1914 by musketry instructor Sergeant Instructor Snoxall who placed 38 rounds into a 12-inch-wide target at 300 yards in one minute. When people still wonder whether Lee Harvey Oswald could really have made those difficult shots from the sixth floor of the Book Depository then S.I. Snoxall would nod and say *Yes. Yes he could.*

There is a well-documented story of German attackers being repelled by what they thought was heavy machine gun fire when in fact it was a group of trained riflemen armed with Lee Enfields.

The German equivalent, the G98 Mauser, compared very favourably to the SMLE but the Germans themselves confessed to preferring the Lee Enfield. Although the Mauser had slightly greater accuracy at distance the SMLE held twice as many rounds, was lighter, made a louder bang, and the British cartridges were effectively the dreaded dum-dum bullets in all but name, in that the point was liable to split on impact and spread within the body.

The musketry course itself involved firing 250 rounds at ranges from between 100, 500 and 600 yards. As a mere private and new recruit Wor Geordie would, by the end of the course, be expected to hit a target 15 times at 100 yards within a minute.

They learned not to jerk the trigger and spoil the shot; they learned to squeeze so smoothly on the outbreath that a farthing balanced on the foresight protector would stay there. If they were good, they got a few extra pennies a day; if they were excellent, they got a whole 6d. (In the reality almost all of them complained about never being paid the right amount, no matter how many skills they accrued.)

He would have to keep the rifle with him at all times and having a dirty weapon would make him liable for Field Punishment No. 2. This could mean fines, confinement to quarters or heavy fatigues. These often involved running around the fields with the rifle held above your head while yelling to the world that you were a particular aspect of female anatomy that many of them had not yet explored.

There were five ranges at Whitburn. One 40 yards long for side arms, and four for rifles (one of 600 yards, and three of 500 yards).

The 40 yards range was the sole preserve of the officers who practised there with their Mark VI Webley Revolvers which, although very powerful and with a huge kick, were only effective or accurate at up to 50 yards. That might not seem very much but they were just as effective as the Colt Walker 1847s used by the Outlaw Josey Wales, and you could even fit them with a bayonet. These were sometimes given to trench raiders, tank crews and machine-gun teams regardless of rank, so it is possible that Geordie might have fired one when he got to Flanders.

In the later years of the war when experienced officers were needed in France, elderly people were brought out of retirement to train the men. Some of these men were often over sixty and brought with them experience that might have been relevant in India 30 years before, but was almost useless now. There are, sadly, all too many stories by recruits of the utterly useless training they were given which prepared them not one bit for Flanders. Yet let's assume that, like J.B. Priestley, Geordie was one of the luckier ones and had top rate instructors – because he must have had something going for him if he survived at the Front for three years.

In terms of sheer fitness there was probably a lot to improve upon. Some of the Physical Training instructors noted that while the miners, for example, were very strong and could dig five foot deep trenches faster than anyone had dug before, they had no 'wind', no stamina for a long run.

In those days no-one went jogging. Certainly not in Geordie's home town. No joggers were glimpsed in Ashington until the late 1980s and they were all seen as a bit weird because some of them didn't even drink alcohol, and you sort of crossed the street when you saw them coming. So right from the start, to toughen them up, the new recruits went on route marches starting at eight miles a day and then building up very quickly to fifteen and twenty-five miles, and in what was termed 'full marching order' – carrying full pack and rifle. It was one way to weed them out.

Marching speed had been calculated at being 98 yards per minute, or three miles an hour, marching in columns of four abreast. They would get a six minute halt every hour. After the very first of these, recruits would know all about blisters and how to lance them, and would become desperate to use the 'sweet pea' method to soften their boots that very night.

Often they were encouraged to sing. Some of the southern battalions in other regiments were known to warble, when marching through small villages or anywhere they were likely to shock, the immortal lines: "Do your balls swing low?/Do they jingle to and fro?" But I couldn't 'hear' our 6th Battalion Northumberland Fusiliers doing that one. They had to burst into Geordie songs appropriate for marching that 98 yards a minute so I decided to do some field work of my own.

As part of my convalescence after having half of my arse removed I was supposed to build up my walking distances every day. In fact, since the über-Geordie had come into my head I'd spent most of my time hunched over the keyboard and farting a lot. So I started off to the local garden centre about a mile away and tried to time my walk with 'The Keel Row':

O, weel may the keel row,
  The keel row, the keel row,
O weel may the keel row
  That my laddie's in.

But that never matched any kind of marching rhythm, and I must have looked as if I was playing that old kids' game of not stepping on cracks else something bad would happen.

So then I tried that well-known Geordie love song 'Cushie Butterfield' with the chorus that would melt any woman's heart:

She's a big lass an' a bonny lass,
An' she likes her beer;
An', they call her Cushy Butterfield,
An' ah wish she waz here.

Better, but a little bit too sprightly, and it had me prancing up and down the pavement like one of those Lipizzaner horses doing imperceptibly points-winning things in the Olympic dressage events.

Then I got it, and you can try this yourself because it will make your left foot strike the pavement infallibly on the beat and you'll be belting along four abreast with the lads of the 6th Battalion as I was, singing 'The Lambton Worm.'

> One Sunda mornin Lambton went
> a-fishing in the weir;
> An' catched a fish upon his heuk
> He thowt leuk't varry queer.
> But wadna kind ov fish it was
> Young Lambton cudna tell
> So he pulled the heuk from oot the gob
> An' hoyed it doon the well.
>
> (ye bugger!)
>
> Whisht! lads, haad ya gobs,
> Ah'll tell ye aall an aaful story,
> Whisht! lads, haad ya gobs,
> Ah'll tell ye 'boot the worm.

If you've got the avatar of Geordie nicely in your psyche by now then this is best marching song of them all you'll be able to make those 98 yards a minute effortlessly.

Whimsy apart, there were two genuine marching songs recorded by the Reverend Wilfrid Callin of the 4th Battalion who was there when they first went to war. He wrote in his rather moving tribute *When the Lantern of Hope Burned Low*.

"Going to battle? Of course we were!" he wrote: "Sufficient unto the day is the evil thereof, so sing, sing, sing! And what songs:"

> There's a moose in oor back hoose,
> Pit lie idle, pit lie idle.

And also the one which has survived today:

Good-bye-ee! Good-bye-ee!
Wipe the tear, baby dear, from your eye-ee!

Apart from the marching in boots there were all those exercises wearing what the Geordies always called sandshoes, that later became part of the 'Physical Training' regimes in all schools: sprints, 440 yds, 880 yds. Push ups, squat thrusts, star jumps, leap-frog, high jumps, log races, long jumps, hurdling, boxing and wrestling – and the inter-company football matches. Apart from the officers no-one was much interested in rugby or even understood it.

Their daily route was quite simple:

6.30 they would have Reveille, being woken by the bugler.
7.15 they would have PT.
8.00 they would have a quick breakfast followed by business of the day in Orderly Room and then:
9.00-10.30 they would be on the parade ground square bashing, learning how to march in step, turn, salute, and do all those soldierly things we've all seen but can't put names to.
11.00-12.30 more drill.
1.00p.m. they would have Dinner.[52]
2.00-3.30pm they would be on parade again.
3.45-4.15 they would have a Lecture, and this could be about anything from the new signalling techniques, how to use the telephone machines, bomb making, map-reading, strangling techniques, and all those tips on personal hygiene that could mean life, death or deformity within the trenches if they were ignored.
5.00 would be tea.
9.30 the bugler would play First Post.
10.00 he would tootle Second Post.
10.15 Lights out.

In the first few weeks they were given training by Battalion, Company or Platoon. They were taught to act and move together on the word of command, almost without thinking, so that 900 men became like drones.

---

52 The Geordie eating regime was always: Breakfast, Dinner (noon-ish), Tea (around 4pm) and a cooked meal at Supper (8ish).

Then came the moment when they tried to teach each man individually the real work of a soldier in the field. Their aim – and the instructors emphasised this strongly – was to teach each man *to think and act for himself*. This was underlined in the training manuals: it might be a shock to the mentality of the officers' caste system but was a very necessary thing in time of war.

The manual went on to insist this didn't mean that a soldier should be taught to act without orders. Oh no. 'He should be taught that when given an order, say, to advance when in the firing line, he should be able to take advantage of the ground in his line of advance of line. He should learn to see what is cover, and understand the use and abuse of cover.'

Well, that was the theory as written up by desk-wallahs whose experience of advancing under fire was almost non-existent, and certainly hadn't involved machine guns.

> You will get stupid men to deal with. As far as you can, keep your own temper, and in dealing with a stupid man, don't bully or rag him – take extra pains with him. On no account be sarcastic and don't hold any man up to the ridicule of his comrades...[53]

To be fair though, when looking at the very best of the training regimes it's hard to see how they could have improved them, given the knowledge available. Even the endless drill, the marching, inevitably has the effect of making a large body of men act and almost think as One, and this was always going to develop the team spirit and sense of belonging.

And then there was bayonet practice. Infantrymen did this with padded jackets and 'rifles' with spring-loaded plungers instead of actual blades. This was taught as if it was a science. Although not many bayonet instructors had really killed with one, they were allowed to imply they had done so often. As we've all seen it done in many documentaries, the soldiers attacked either hanging or prone

---

53 From a training lecture given to officers. Quoted in Lyn Macdonald's *1914-1918* p 56.

sandbags which were marked to represent the vulnerable areas of the Hun's body: face, chest, lower abdomen, balls.

The best possible thrust with the vicious twelve inch blade should ideally be against the throat, as this would make a fatal wound on penetrating, and being near the eyes would make the bastard 'funk'. You didn't need to drive it all the way in because then it was often difficult to withdraw. At such times, you would have to fire a round into your victim to clear the obstruction.

"Howay Geordie man!" you can hear the instructors cry. "Four inches is enough. Even your lass doesn't want the whole twelve!"

In many ways this science they taught was a bit of a con. The idea of 'bayonet fighting' was more in the realm of Douglas Fairbanks in 1917 silents like *The Modern Musketeer* than what actually happened. Although many soldiers in all armies were indeed killed with the blades, there was neither art nor science involved but a few seconds of frantic butchery.

The main purpose of the bayonet practice was to get the men to scream and shout and generally learn, on a sedate English field, how to be a maniac.

For many of them, this would be their first time away from home, their first experience of life without their Mams.[54] Homesickness was not a problem for our Geordie because he gone through all that years before, when he had left Newcastle to start afresh in Ashington. It was a real agony for some of the younger ones.

Yet some of them also found that they were now getting the best meals they ever had – though they'd never dare tell their Mams that. Throughout the war, when Germans over-ran British trenches and took whatever they could find, they were often dismayed by the sheer quality of food that the Tommies had, as compared to themselves.

One of the main culture shocks was in meeting, on equal terms, a very wide variety of men from other backgrounds. Miners mixed with farm hands; milk men with railway workers; shopkeepers with navvies, suddenly all crammed together into freezing cold huts or tents and being made to act as One.

---

54 Always difficult for young Geordies. I maintain that when Paul Gascoigne was a little fat boy living with his Mam, he was the greatest footballer in the world.

Of course it was almost compulsory that ex-public schoolboys should immediately become officers, and the rank and file took that for granted. The playwright R.C. Sherriff who would fight in the same battlefields as our man and then went on to create a Virtual Reality of the Western Front with his play *Journey's End* wrote with astonishment about his own attempts to get a commission:

> "School?" enquired the adjutant. I told him and his face fell. He took up a printed list and searched through it. "I'm sorry," he said, "but I'm afraid it isn't a public school." I was mystified. I told him that my school, though small, was a very old and good one – founded, I said by Queen Elizabeth in 1567. The adjutant was not impressed. "I'm sorry," he repeated. "But our instructions are that all applications for commissions must be selected from the recognised public schools and yours is not among them."[55]

Some men became officers without even an interview. George Gillet was offered a commission while playing cricket with a colonel. He was told that if he wanted to bring along any of his friends from Harrow, they could also have a commission.

Toward the end of the war, out of sheer necessity and amid much internal soul-searching within the higher echelons, it was eventually possible to be promoted from within the ranks. Until then the privates and the NCOs simply had to play up, play up and play the game. With very mixed results when it came to leadership.

There was a piece of research done about Ashington once, in the late 1960s, because it was seen as almost a uni-class society. There was some truth in that. We never met what might be termed and recognised as the 'upper' classes, and even many of the people occupying 'middle' class positions were ex-miners or the wives of such. The relatively posh kids, as we saw them, lived in the small number of council houses with their gardens and indoor toilets and hot water. Some of them had central heating. But at least we all had radio and our 405 line tellies and could see how the other portions of society lived and could study them from afar with some bemusement but not the slightest sense of envy. Thanks to this, we understood the English that the rest of the world was speaking. In 1914 or 1915 when the Geordies went to their training camps, some of the officers must have sounded incomprehensible.

---

55 Quoted in: http://www.spartacus.schoolnet.co.uk/FWWcamps.htm

So when the Geordies left their homes and Mams and went to camp it would have brought a culture shock in both directions. In their brilliant book *Tyneside Scottish* Graham Stewart and John Sheen quote a new officer's bewilderment when he tried to relate to the strange men he had come to command:

> What did puzzle me very much at first was the Tyneside speech. Many a time when attempting to talk to a man in the ranks I knocked up against a, to me, perfectly unintelligible reply and I must confess that despite my best endeavours, though I improved to some extent, I have never yet reached any degree of proficiency in the language of the Tyne.

This is funny at first, but if you were a young Geordie infantryman whose section had just been shot to pieces on the battlefield and wanted to explain the situation to an officer, you would want him to understand what you were saying.

In all the accounts I have read the ordinary Geordie soldier was quite happy to follow officers from within his own Northumbrian or County Durham kind, whether they were public school toffs or not. Like those miners I mentioned earlier going dewy eyed at the Duchess of Northumberland, it was almost a feudal thing among them.

Which brings our avatar – almost – to that moment when he was fully trained and about to entrain to France – where he would receive an even more intensive level of training at one of the Bullrings before being sent to the Front. Each man there would by this time have received a little missive from Lord Kitchener himself to prepare himself for this foreign realm. It read:

> Keep constantly on your guard against any excesses. In this new experience you may find temptations both in wine and women. You must entirely resist both temptations, and while treating all women with perfect courtesy, you should avoid any intimacy.

Robert Graves in his classic *Goodbye to all That* noted that all his men wanted to lose their virginity before they died, but at least

Private George M. Richardson didn't have that pressure. When he joined up full time he was, in the eyes of the lads around, almost an old man at the age of 33. He knew all about sex, and was probably happy to share his knowledge with the doomed virgins around him, becoming as One as they marched together, ate together, crapped in fields together, and were about to share trenches and fight together far from their tribal lands.

As I have the whole virtual battalion lined up in my head now, I have to say they look magnificent: hard and handsome, somewhat worried about the future but full of hope. And I start to understand at least something of this Why to end all Whys.

Even after that first day of the Somme Offensive on July 1st when they were cut to shreds, they still saw that they had a job to do and wanted to finish it. It wasn't that they didn't have the gumption to start a revolt. After all, the brief mutiny at the Bullring in Étaples was led by a Northumberland Fusilier. No, they saw themselves as fighting to protect us back home, all the Mams and Dads and all the bairns, to try to keep us safe in our beds and the darkness from taking us. On July 2nd, with the chaos of battle being what it is, they had no sense of it being an unparalleled military disaster. It was a 20 mile front. For all they knew, the other divisions were half way to Berlin by then. They'd taken a hammering, certainly, but they'd done their bit on the day, and intended to carry on doing so until Fritzie was finished.

There's more that they're still not telling me but I expect I'll have to get them to France before I learn that.

As I watch them in their final parade on English soil there is rain falling and a chill wind from the North Sea. They stamp their boots in the mud as they turn and send splashes up their puttees. They are, as my mother might have said, giving her highest praise, 'canny bits of lads' and I feel humbled by their presence in my mind.

Though I'm not sure I'd trust my daughters with any of them.

8

STRANGERS IN A STRANGE LAND

IF THE 6th Battalion Northumberland Fusiliers were learning to act as one before setting off for France, the newly repaired watch was splitting me into several personalities, each one flowing back and forth through time.

In the eyes of my children this talismanic object, which absorbs my waking moments, is known to them as Dad's Watch.

To me, even before I took formal almost apostolic possession, it was also Dad's Watch.

And during the long years he kept it hidden in a plastic purse at the back of a drawer, far from his own troubled conscience and difficult wife, it was Dad's Watch in my own dad's mind too.

These days I don't know where I begin and the other Dads end. Or is it the other way around? I'm only grateful to The Mam that I was not called George Matthew Richardson also, or I might have disintegrated long ago.

So where am I now? Who am I now?

As I write this it is the summer of 2012, but also of 1944. Grandad is upstairs in his bedroom, sitting in a chair, looking out of the window across the football fields. The Jarmins couldn't get him with their Mausers, Maxims, *minen* and Whizz-bangs but the Wild Woodbine cigarettes that they used in the trenches as currency finally did for him. He is in great pain from cancer of the oesophagus but sometimes whispers to people that he had known far worse at Ypres, and he probably did. Rum helps, and reminds him of the tots they all got before a battle and sometimes after one. The watch is on his lap and he polishes it with a large and slightly grimy hanky, remembering the care he once lavished – had to lavish on his rifle.

The heavy blackout curtains for the window are pulled aside. There used to be tape across the glass in case of German bombing, but there are only desultory raids these days on the submarine pens at Blyth, five miles away. As an old soldier who has keenly followed the news, he would lecture to anyone who would listen that after Stalingrad last year, and the Normandy invasions this year, them Jarmins would soon be finished. Again.

The front door out onto Alexandra Road slams shut and shivers the windowpanes. It reminds him of the sound of a bullet hitting a sandbag at the back of a trench. He leans forward in his chair and sees his first son Geordie – now known as Big Geordie – walking hand in hand with his new and pregnant wife Francy. They seem happy, and well matched. Soon, they plan to move in next door at number 71 but he thinks this might be a mistake, as Jinny doesn't think Francy is good enough for her son. It's not a good tactic on the part of the Bevin Boy to have two powerful women so close to each other, and both vying for his attention: it would be like trench warfare between the two adjoining back yards, with dangerous stuff flying back and forward.

He looks at the watch, peers at his distorted reflection in the case. He pretends to others that the watch is a bit of a joke. But its inscription, and the little ceremony they had for him at Ashington Town Hall, is the only proof he has that his war was worthwhile.

Although the watch isn't broken, exactly, he cannot wind it any more. The mechanism is jammed. One of his bairns would have overwound it when his back was turned. He can't afford to get it fixed and only hopes that this Big Geordie, as they all call him, will look after it when he – now known as Old Geordie – is dead. He is too shy to approach the lad and ask. He still doesn't understand why his first son won't talk to him, and it hurts. He blames Jinny but wouldn't dare tell her that: anything for peace and quiet. There wasn't much he didn't know about total warfare on the Western Front, but he couldn't manage his wife at all.

(Although maybe I'm just projecting into a previous generation the internecine destruction wrought by own parents, demonising my old granny as we demonised the Germans. At the end of my own life, when I go stumbling across the spiritual equivalent of No Man's Land toward those broad sunlit uplands that we all aspire toward, I'll keep an eye out for Jinny and make it up to her. Honest.)

It had cost £400 to get the watch fixed. A bargain, I thought, once I stopped whimpering. And an odd thing happened when it was ticking again. Although I'd approached my numerous cousins to ask about our mutual grandparents, none of them knew what had happened to Long Lost Cousin Billy, except that his father (our Uncle Bill) had died in America many years before. He had emigrated with his family to America in the early 1950s, and almost immediately severed all contact with his family here.

Over many years, long before the internet existed, I had made desultory efforts to find that lost branch of our family but the names William/Bill/Richardson are so common that I got nowhere.

It was Wor Pat who remembered something about this Uncle Bill, Dad's younger brother, the one who had served in the Guards during World War II and was wounded at Tobruk. She recalled that he had been named William *Haig* Richardson – which at very least which shows that our grandfather had nothing but admiration for that general and his tactics.

So I added the name 'Haig' to my search, googled accordingly and found him – or rather his son – on the first hit: William Haig Richardson *Jr*.

He had posted on an obscure site that he had grown up in America without his dysfunctional British parents ever talking about their background, and concluded:

> We left England for the US in 1952 and I had my 2nd birthday on the SS Mauritania mid ocean.
>
> I have never known another family member, never seen a grandparent, aunt, uncle, etc. and now in failing health myself, I have set upon a "bucket list" of sorts to locate another who may remember my family. With luck I hope to return home for a visit that is now well overdue.

His father, with whom he had a difficult relationship, did once mention that he had a brother who was a coal miner, in a small town called Northumberland, near Cumberland.

Bloody Hell I thought, the hair on my neck prickling. *This is Long Lost Cousin Billy!*

Who is of course, now, Finally Found Cousin Bill, who had spent thirty years in Indianapolis as a Deputy Sheriff. Our paths must have crossed many times when I was over there, and he might well have had cause to arrest me at least a few of those times if truth be told. The dynamic between his mum and dad and himself was eerily similar to what I had known. But:

I have our grandfather's medals, he said. *Do you want them?*

At some point after opening the watch and finally getting it fixed, I became other people. We all do when we search for and find those lost mechanisms of family that we don't even know exist, and set wheels turning that we never quite understand. Somehow that involved finding Cousin Bill, who couldn't even remember posting on that website; and Pat gifting me the middle name of 'Haig' although afterward she was surprised by that, as she couldn't remember ever knowing that, or even telling me.

Just as I've never understood the inner mechanical workings of Dad's magickal watch, or the importance of the jewels, by the same token I will never fathom the inner workings of Family.

Yet by possessing it I became my Dad and my Grandad. And part of this was caused by that maddening chorus of *There's a moos in oor back hoos/pit lie idle, pit lie idle* from the genuine marching song of the Northumberland Fusiliers.

Being hearing-impaired and with little grasp of tune, I've always joked that I stopped listening to music when Boney M broke up. Yet I've got an infallible sense of rhythm and my various efforts to make this arrhythmic couplet come alive seemed to start something vibrating in harmony. Slowly, in the night, I became a silent presence among them all, an exiled Geordie spirit loose within the Geordiedom of an era which formed me.

Eh? Calm doon son.
I'm okay dad, really.
Ah knaa that. Ah just want tae learn what happened next.
You never left this country did you?
Ah nivver had the chance.
Where would you have gone?
Whey France of course. The owld bugger med it seem like Butlins...

When the original First Battalion Northumberland Fusiliers of the Regular Army left for France to join the British Expeditionary

Force on 13th August 1914 they did so in secrecy and silence. They got on board the SS Norman at Southampton and disembarked at Le Havre where they were met by a minute but very alert French boy scout who guided them six miles to their very first camp at Epremesnil. This distance would, later, have been nothing to the newly-trained and superbly fit 6th Battalion of Wor Geordie, but these Regular Army men hadn't done any active soldiering in a very long time and some of them found it difficult.

Yet they were fêted every step of the way. Roadsides were crowded with girls and little children, and stern old women in the fields who twirled imaginary moustaches to indicate the Kaiser, pointing to the frontier then drawing their hands across their throats. In Belgium it seemed to be largely strong young men who cried out 'Forward my brave ones!' though the lads noted that they didn't seem to be in any hurry to join them. Still, the natives were all grateful that professional soldiers had arrived to free them from the oncoming German tyranny.

These Northumberland Fusiliers first met their enemy of the next four years at Mariette, on the Condé Canal. With Belgians to the left of them, French to the right, a line was created between the armies that sometimes wavered but never entirely broke, stretching from the North Sea to Switzerland, for the rest of the war.

As the Geordies still say about such circumstances, they could neither heck nor gee. And to the horror of General Haig the shovel became as important a part of the soldier's equipment as the rifle. So his precious cavalry was never going to play a part in the grand schemes of things at all.

It became a war of attrition from then on.

When Wor Geordie and his War Geordies first left Southampton the following year, 1915, they were in a small convoy of other troop ships. For most of them, unless they had been fishermen in civilian life, this was their first time at sea with all the attendant problems of sea-sickness and danger from submarines. They were escorted across by the comforting presence of an airship under the aegis of the RNAS.[56] Some of the Geordies might have seen the Zeppelins

---

56 Royal Naval Air Service

when they raided, and even glimpsed a few – a very few – heavier than air machines also, but the sight of a sky full of both as they approached France was almost eerie, like something imagined in the mad books of that Jules Vorn.

The role of the airship, of course, was to act as a spotter. If a submarine was sighted the airship would alert the nearby destroyers, those greyhounds of the sea, some of which had been built at Armstrong's shipyards, and these would dash over and plaster the area with depth charges while the troopships made a run for it. Allied shipping losses in the Great War were staggering. Germany almost won the war through the effectiveness of their submarines alone.

When they disembarked in Le Havre this once sleepy port was now a maelstrom of high-tech military activity, but the French welcome that the 1st Battalion had experienced a year before had long since dissipated and the only words that the children seemed to use were 'Fuck off Tommy'. Numerous Fusiliers commented in later years that the French had been the most hateful, unhelpful, unpleasant and most ignorantest folk they had ivver met.

Then again, in those parts of France and Belgium which now formed the Western Front, it seemed that we had liberated them back to the Stone Age. By the time the British Army finally left France nearly 2000 villages had been totally destroyed, and a greater number than that just completely ruined, not to mention thousands of miles of road and rail connections, 20 thousand factories, and 4 million hectares of land made waste, often for decades. A number of French and Belgians would later wonder if it would have been better just to let the Germans through to the coast and take over completely.

Both Germany and Britain made efforts to give their largely uneducated infantry some basic communication skills with friend and foe. The *landsers*, as the former thought of themselves, were taught phonetic phrases such as:

Honds opp ju fohl (hands up you fool!) At the entrance of a British dug-out, if they didn't want to throw in a stick grenade they might call out: *Is anibodi inseid?* And then call out: *Kom ohl aut, quick quick*. If anyone did finally appear it would be *Honds opp, kom on Tomy*.

Oddly enough, there was little point in giving similar instructions to the Tommies because not all Germans spoke German. Unification within that country had only occurred 40 years before, and there were numerous languages embedded within its new borders, including a 'lower class' version known as *platsdeutsch* which was far removed from the High German of the ruling classes. Some of the German states loathed the dominant Prussians far more than the Tommies they were forced to fight, and if it hadn't been for the war the Geordies might have got on very well with the Low German *platsdeutsch* speakers.

The British educators in the War Department devised their own special booklet called 'What You Want to Say in French and How To Say it' although it was clearly pitched at officers with phrases like: 'Please can you help me billet my men?' or 'Can I have some water for my horse?'

However the Tommies with typical delight shortened the whole system, starting with the all-embracing shoulder-hands-eyebrow raise which could express phrases as diverse as:

I am not surprised!
I don't know. Perhaps.
I really don't understand a word you're saying.
I don't know who the father might be.

And then there was *La Gaire* (La Guerre – the War) which could be used for:

I've had enough
Yes I shot your horse with my Lewis gun but…
I didn't mean to crap in your helmet
It's not my fault bonny lass.

Without exception they all talked about having a *bon* pint, a *bon* cup of tea, a *bon* night out. Or if you were an officer in the Northumberland Fusiliers you could even try your hand at rendering into French such Geordie phrases as *Ah'm hard, me man* to become: *Je suis dur, moi homme.*[57]

---

[57] (Cousin Bill in the US: when Geordies end a sentence with *man* it is a means of emphasis, said very quickly, almost biting it out, and has no gender association. So you could say to your wife (and many do): *Oh bonny lass, Ah luv ye man!*)

So one effect of all this was that Geordie quickly became quadri-lingual.

Eh?

1. He spoke his native dialect, which sounds like a chain-saw in its purest form.
2. He spoke 'High Geordie', called in my day the 'taalkin' on the telephone voice', which was first unleashed on the nation in the television series 'When the Boat Comes In'.
3. When speaking to officers he might try for Proper English, which is when he tried to pronounce words 'correctly' but retaining the same Geordie rhythms, producing something that sounds either Irish or Norwegian.
4. And he mastered all this French stuff, nae bother.

They tried to teach me French at school. I had four years of it. And while I, a Francophile, could say with confidence that my aunt's handbag was not on the ceiling, mais non, but her pen was certainement on the floor, I could not have ordered a cup of coffee in France itself.

The lads of the Fighting Fifth however seized upon the new *linguae franca* with all the delight that other Tommies used, and it took me a long time to realise that I had had heard fragments of this in the Grand Hotel in Ashington 50 years later.

"Sand Fairy Anne" said one of the oldest gadgies to me when I spilt some beer on his Sporting Pink newspaper.[58] He looked at me pityingly and must have wondered what tribe I belonged to, with my shoulder length hair, two-tone purple loons and kaleidoscopic yellow shirt with a collar that I could have used as a hang-glider.

"Eh?" I responded, already *homaging* my Dad, although in those days I thought of it as a private piss-take.

"It doesn't matter Jacky, it doesn't matter."

I didn't know that he was literally interpreting the phrase for me, this being the Great War's rendition of *Ça ne fait rien*.

And that was another thing. If they didn't know your name up there in Ashington the very old fellas would call you Jacky. I didn't

---

[58] This was not a gay contact magazine but a newspaper printed on very thin, pink paper which came out 20 minutes after the football had ended, with all the results.

mind, because it sounded much better than the wimpy 'Alan'. But could that have come from a time when they called all strangers in a strange land Jacques?

"Napoo crisps," said his pal, and they shared that vaguely shitey look that people have when they use language to exclude.

I thought at the time it might have been pit jargon but I see now these were men who would certainly have known Grandad from his many years behind the bar, and may even have fought with him in France.

And that word *Napoo* was probably the mightiest of all, coming from *Il n'y en a plus* meaning: There is no more of it.

Napoo money
Napoo Fritzie
Napoo jig-a-jig bonny lass?

And I have this irresistible fantasy that somewhere near Ypres today is a man my age who once sat in a bar in his teens listening to the latest hits from that young English import Helen Shapiro, who became bigger over there than in her native land. He sipped his pastis while listening to the contemptuous *les vieux* around him using such phrases as: *Nae frites ce soir pet? Nae vin blanc? Haddaway!* and wondering what manner of men from the ancient of days might have left behind such a legacy.

After his battalion arrived at Le Havre he would have travelled onward by train to various railheads behind the front. The officers had carriages of course, while the ordinary soldiers were squeezed into covered trucks that were primarily designed for horses. Because of the inherent chaos of the war, damage to tracks up the line, and the attendant build-up of traffic, a journey of a hundred miles could take up to three days. If the men wanted to relieve themselves they had to leap off whenever it came to a halt and scramble to get back on again. That might have been undignified to the new lads but the ex-miners wouldn't have been fazed by such things: there were no netties at the coal face.

By the time Geordie arrived in France almost everyone had to go up to the line, as they called the Front, via one of the Bullrings. There were actually several of these dotted across the British area for the further training of the Tommy, including large bases near Rouen, Harfleur, Le Havre and Étaples, and they each contained the training compounds, hospitals and convalescent areas, canteens, and endless rows of tents for the privates and small huts or sometimes much better for their officers.

Everything that Geordie learned in St George's Drill Hall and then at Boldon Camp was now cranked up to a higher level. In some cases the training was so intense that many preferred being at the Front to suffering the wrath and sadism of the NCO instructors.

These were known as Canaries because of the yellow armbands they wore and were loathed not simply because of their vicious methods, but because they themselves, and their often tactless officers, had never been anywhere near the battlefields.

The training was so real that stretcher bearers were always on hand to carry away the casualties. They did assault courses with full pack, jumping into and out of 8' trenches, running across a chaos of water-filled shell holes, going over under or through masses of barbed wire while having live ammunition fired above their heads and pelted with whatever missiles the Canary had at hand, whether it was bully beef tins to represent a grenades or heavy rocks to give a hint of shrapnel. And if they didn't do it right, they did it again. And again. And if they were exhausted then too bad, they would *really* be punished then.

Like medieval knights they were made to train and fight with levels of ammunition and equipment far heavier than they would probably carry in real conflict so that – in theory – they could move with ease in their proper kit.

They learned how to kill with their bare hands. They learned how to fight with knives, clubs, bayonets and – very handy in enclosed spaces – their entrenching tools. They learned to use, without conscience or hesitation, every trick, weapon or technique to stop their opponent.

"Ye want tae see yer bairns again Geordie? It's them or you, remember that. Noo dae it again, harder!"

If we really want to see the conflict through Geordie's eyes then we have to become aware of all those items of war that became as familiar to him as all the pots and pans, cups and saucers in Jinny's kitchen. And we can start by looking a simple defensive device which, along with the machine gun, transformed warfare forever. It was cheap, idiot-proof, could be set up in minutes and could turn a battlefield certainty into an absolute disaster. Geordie had seen its cousin many times in the fields around Ashington, but its only purpose there had been to keep the coos from straying. Here in France, the Germans took **Barbed Wire** into another dimension.

This wire was laid in thick coils over 3 feet high and fixed in position by stakes, often in parallel rows. Barbed wire was the cheapest, simplest, most devastating defensive aspect of the war. Time and time again British attacks failed because the men just could not get through the enemy wire which often resisted – quite literally – tons of high explosive directed at it.

I'll come back to that later and also mention how it was the lassies at Armstrong's Factory that got some of the blame for that. So they learned about the wire, and how to go over it and under it, though in truth no-one ever mastered it until the new-fangled tanks just dragged the stuff aside in the later years of the war.

Then there was the device which was almost the malign complement of the wire, because the latter was often laid in ways that would funnel attackers toward the withering fire of the:

Machine Gun. The Vickers Machine Gun was made in Armstrong's factory by Geordie's own relatives. They were heavy devices and needed a whole panoply of men, mountings, carriages and supplies to keep them in action. Although only a few men would volunteer to specialise they got 6d a day extra pay because it was known as the Suicide Club. Neither Fritz nor Tommy would show any mercy to any machine gunner they might capture. They would not be allowed to surrender. I'm sure my Dad told me that Wor Geordie had been a machine-gunner, though there is no evidence of that.

The early guns were water cooled and would still overheat relatively quickly (sometimes within two minutes), so large supplies of water would need to be on hand in the heat of a battle. And, when these ran out, it was said to be not unknown for a machine gun crew to solve the problem by urinating into the jacket. (Though I don't believe that myself. It would take a rare man who, in the terror of the battlefield, would be able to stand up, whip his todger out and maintain a steady and directed flow onto his gun.) Later ones were air-cooled and these were much more reliable, although they could still jam frequently, especially in hot conditions or when used by someone who was panicking. Consequently machine guns would often be grouped together to maintain a constant defence.

These early Vickers machine guns could fire 400-600 rounds per minute, a figure that was to more than double by the war's end, with rounds fed via a fabric belt or a metal strip. It could cut a man in half like a scythe.

It took a long time for the British High Command to accept the machine gun as a valuable and pre-eminent weapon. These were the souls, remember, who had insisted in 1912 that the lance should still be a part of the cavalryman's weaponry. The lance! In fact it took the wholesale slaughter of British soldiers by German Maxim machine guns to persuade them otherwise. On the opening day of the Somme Offensive that we keep coming back to, the great majority of British casualties were caused by machine gun fire.

However, by the time of the British attack on High Wood on 24th August 1916, the Vickers had proved itself, and even General Haig and the (by now deposed) General Sir John French had begun to accept that – perhaps – cavalry was no match against machine guns after all, and if they wanted to win this bally war they'd better equip their men with the best guns they could get. At the battle of High Wood it is estimated that ten Vickers fired in excess of one million rounds over a twelve hour period. Estimates of their equivalent, accurate, rifle firepower varied, with some estimating a single machine gun to be worth as many as 60-100 rifles.

They also learned how to use:

The Mills Bomb. This was virtually identical to the modern hand grenade and were designed to kill by fragmentation rather than explosive force. A strong thrower could hurl them, overarm, for nearly 40 yards.

The Trench Mortar. Although there were numerous versions the main one was a lightweight tube that was angled off vertical to lob a projectile in a high arc over a short range, down into the German trench – probably about 800 yards away. The bombs were spherical, weighed 60 lbs, and were mounted on two-inch steel tubular stalks. The Geordies called them 'toffee apples'. While they were highly effective they tended to blast their stalks right back at their firers, like boomerangs.

And then there was the:

Lewis Gun, which the instructors in their purity would call an automatic rifle but which was a machine gun to everyone else. This was more popular with soldiers because it was lighter (one quarter the weight of a Vickers), and could be carried into battle by one man. It had similar rate of fire but its magazines only held 47 bullets, so you needed two men with the gunner to carry extra magazines, and also give them support in the isolated positions they had to maintain.

And then they learned about:

Gas. The ex-miners among the Fighting Fifth were less intimidated by this than the others. They made a living underground with their special gas-alerting lamps and had canaries in cages which keeled over when gas was present; so you can imagine they had some fun with the very idea of those Canaries in the Bullring.

Different types of gas were used during the war, ranging from a simple sneezing agent which many didn't even notice, through to the dreadful chlorine, phosgene and mustard gases which could cause dreadful injuries. When this was first used it confirmed in the minds of the astonished and disgusted world that they really were fighting against Huns, and by god *someone* had to stop them!

In the early days the only defence suggested was to use towels or even sanitary pads soaked in urine to absorb the toxic vapours, although this had little effect. Later still the boffins developed 'smoke helmets', which were grey flannel bags impregnated with hexamine and glycerine, with two eyepieces and a rubber mouthpiece. As the gas being used became more sophisticated and ever more lethal, so did the gas masks, and newcomers to the Bullrings would be given time in the Gas Rooms to make sure they fitted their own kit quickly and properly.

And finally they learned about:

The Trench and trench-building. They'd done a bit in England, but here was the real thing. For a tribe that made a living as troglodytes, the science of trench-building and living in such was not a great shock to the Geordies' system. In the type of warfare which had rapidly evolved – and the Jarmins dug in forst! – they didn't really have much choice.

The ideal trench, if that's not an absurd term, was 7 feet deep and 3 feet wide at the bottom, slightly wider at the top. Along the front and rear edges it had raised areas known as the parapet and parados respectively. At the side facing the enemy there was a raised piece known as the fire-step, from which they could stand and shoot. The trenches were reinforced, where they could, with corrugated iron, timber, wickerwork, or wire netting. The bottoms were floored with duckboards to aid movement and also help drain the water.

They became almost scientific. The communication trenches between the front and rear lines were zig-zagged to protect against enfilade fire: that is, bullets or explosions which would otherwise wipe out a whole line of defenders. The front line trench was fashioned similarly. There were passing places, places for latrines, and bombing pits. Their concern was to provide adequate cover while enabling a good field of fire against attacking hordes.

Well, that was the theory.

In reality the Germans had the advantage in that they were, for the most part, on higher ground. From where they dug in at Ypres, for example, every part of the town was visible to them and their guns so that in a short space of time it was shelled into becoming a City of the Dead, and only came alive during the night. Not only did they have a clear sight of the entire British placements but when they used pumps to drain their own trenches of the excess water they could direct it downhill to the already waterlogged British positions.

In many parts of marshy Flanders the water table was only a couple of feet below the surface. If you tried to dig an 8 feet deep trench then 6 feet would just be mud – and so impossible. Then you would have to use sandbags instead and create what were known as breastworks, building a thick wall and going as deep into the mud as was practicable, using the planks known as duck boards to walk along.

In the early stages of the War when those passionate cavalrymen Generals French and Haig still ached for that great surging attack with cavalry, trench-building in the magnificent manner of the Germans was not encouraged: they didn't want the men to get too comfortable in these trenches; they wanted them to *attack attack attack*.

The Germans, however, were by this time happy to *defend defend defend*, and with the higher, dryer ground they were able to create trench systems that were up to 40 feet deep, many with concrete bunkers inserted that were often shell-proof.

When the 6th Battalion first arrived at the front they took over a trench system from the French that was well below the standards they had been taught at the Bullring. Then again, few of the instructors there would have known reality if it had bit them on the arse.

After the Bullrings the Geordies were dropped into trench warfare of the worst kind, right from the start, and many of them would have given anything to be safe and sound back at home within their pits, rather than these shallow scrapes amid a marshy land.

As they had started to do first in St George's Drill Hall, then in Boldon Camp they now found themselves learning about the Arts of War at a far deeper and nastier level. Every man had to be disabused of any notion he might still have regarding life and its inherent fairness. Geordie and his marrers, with all the curious innocence that still marks their tribe, learned things that were not cricket.

There is no doubt that, in normal human terms, many of the Canaries were simple sadists who had found their ideal perch within these training camps, yet in some ways, if you could cope with them then you might have a chance of surviving at the Front. A number of the 'graduates' later spoke very highly of the quality of the training they received, even if it wasn't entirely applicable to the eventual and incredible horror of the real thing.

Étaples was the scene of a famous mutiny, one of only three within the entire British Army. This was not inspired by any sort of socialist class warfare directed at the privileged officer, their NCO lackeys and the general insanity of the war itself. It was in fact the general anger of experienced soldiers outraged by the unfair treatment of a young New Zealander. There was prominent rioting among the Scots and Australian contingent, but the only one eventually tried and shot for actual mutiny was Jesse Short of the 24th Battalion Northumberland Fusiliers.

Most soldiers actually supported the discipline, and when the Canaries and the most supine and indolent of the officers were eventually disbanded and sent to the Front, they felt that true justice had been done.

In truth the Canaries and their doings at the Bullring wouldn't have troubled Wor Geordie too much. He was old enough to know how to play the game, not get noticed and get through the day. Besides, he'd seen enough truly hard men during his time as a barman at Ashington, not to mention Jinny's scary dad, The Hewer, whose respect he was just about winning now. This was all such a far cry from pulling pints and cleaning up after drunkards at the Grand Hotel.

Until he came under German artillery for the first time, this was the best time in his young life.

9

FURTHER OVER THE TOP

For a people who are so deeply attached to their tribal lands, the Geordies are inveterate travellers, and they will tell you: *Where ivver ye gaan ye're sure tae find a Geordie.*

They're not wrong. When I was a very young man, happily doing my wild young man thing in the US, selling my plasma for $10 a pint, writing short articles for small newspapers, doing various odd jobs well below the radar of the IRS,[59] I also spent some time as an actor in a travelling company. We took plays to regions of Appalachia that were so remote they had to pump in the daylight, as they liked to say there. This was long before they made *Deliverance* in those parts, which I've never seen as an action movie with homoerotic undertones but more of a fly-on-the-wall documentary.

We did panto-type shows for children during the day, and a serious play – about World War 1 – in the evenings for adults. Shamefully, I cannot remember the play's name but I had two parts: a devious French padre and – ironically – a young doomed British officer who was worried about going over the top. My passion for the parts was greatly admired, but one critic commented afterward that the skinny dude making the kooky attempt at an English accent kinda spoiled it.

But I was also accosted by a very elderly lady with wax-like, almost translucent skin and great sunken eyes, wearing layers of very frilly pink dresses whose face lit up when she learned that I really was English. She told me that her great-great-grandfather (whom she never knew) had come from the small town of North Umberland, near London in England, where he had once worked in a coal mine, and did I know it? *And would you like some apple pie, Ellen?* she asked.

The point is, this overseas trip would have been meat and drink for Wor Geordie during those crucial (and still safe) years of his early 30s. How else would he ever get to travel? He could catch

---

[59] Internal Revenue Service

the bus to Newbiggin by the Sea, or go to 'Cock and Hen Day' at Morpeth for the Wednesday market when the pubs stayed open all day. Or he might get third class train travel to Newcastle to watch his team play. But with working long hours during a 6 day week no-one had much time to go places. So what did he think when him and the lads of the 6th Battalion first set eyes on Loos and the surrounding area as they headed up to Ypres?

Bliddy hell, lads...it's jist like bliddy Ashington!

The waste heaps around Ashington are all gone now but they were monstrous and massive affairs which created a semi-circle around the northern edges of the town. Everyone called them the Ashington Alps, though Dad always preferred to call them the Mountains of Mourne, with a slight emphasis as if he wanted me to ask why. I knew he wanted me to ask why so I bliddy didn't, did I? (And ye gods but the number of times since I've taken the inner Lewis Gun to pump a few rounds into the young lad I was then!)

Loos was exactly like this, an area of intense mining activity with large waste heaps called either 'crassiers' or 'fosse', and the mines themselves, looking just like the ones at Ashington and Woodhorn Collieries were even called 'puits', which translated exactly as 'pits'. The reports of the officers who had never seen anything like this area show that they weren't from the heart of Geordieland. It would be very difficult terrain militarily, they feared.

The lads who would be on the front line had never really known much different, and it was all a far cry from the continental idyll they might have hoped for.

Although they were soon to fight in Loos too, the ultimate destination for the 149th Brigade was this town called Ypres.

When they finally arrived on the outskirts of that town – which they all learned to pronounce as Wipers – it was April 23rd, St George's Day, which was as special to the regiment in normal times as Christmas Day. These were not normal times.

When these new and inexperienced troops of Geordie's battalions were moved toward that part of the line, their primary role had been to act as reserves. Once the experienced soldiers already in place had dealt with the situation, the Territorials of the Fighting Fifth would move swiftly and seamlessly into their places, as practised again and again at the Bullring.

They were supporting Canadians, who as a body were showing the world what would later be confirmed by Rommel himself 25 years later: that they were among the finest, meanest, toughest fighting men who ever lived.

Brigadier H.R. Sandilands, who wrote the immensely detailed *The Fifth in the Great War,* confessed to the impossibility of writing a definitive account of these days. Because of the situation, reserve units such as Geordie's had been split into fragments and thrown piecemeal into the fight.

As they approached Ypres along a road of splattered trees, past the long grey wall of the emptied Asylum, marching in their columns of four through the square of the town, shells were crashing on or above the cobbled streets, and they got their first taste of shrapnel as it pinged across between the broken buildings. The Cloth Hall and the Cathedral were on fire. The bells kept chiming when bits of flying metal hit them.

Their first casualty was a postman from Ashington called Tommy Rachael who got hit in the leg by something and cried out; "I'm wounded!" This was such a surprise that no-one believed him. The reality of the war hadn't quite sunk in yet. Then somebody noticed the blood pouring down his leg and called out: "Help him! Help him somebody! He's not ganna drop oot! We're the Northummerland Fusiliers!"

The captain was proud of his lads. As they marched along they saw the most ghastly sights of officers and men lying dead and dying by the roadside. "Star shells went up and came crashing down amongst us. Horses lay with broken legs and *still* the men marched steadily. There was no time to attend to the wounded and if your best friend was knocked out you just had to leave him and go on without breaking the column of fours. I was proud of my men; no shouting required, no bullying, only 'Steady lads, steady' and on they came and never looked back..."

They were Northummerland Fusiliers, and fighting for their homeland. They were nivver ganna run.

That was the spirit they entered Ypres with. And it didn't much diminish over the years to come when that rivulet of blood down Tommy's leg became a River Tyne.

Are ye maykin' this up son?
No Dad, everything I write is taken from the experience of somebody within the Northumberland Fusiliers, or connected with them at the time.

By the time they had reached the outskirts of Ypres neither officers nor men had the slightest idea where they were going, or what they were meant to do. They were like all those cowboys in all those Westerns who were told: *Let's head 'em off at the Pass!* But without knowing exactly where the pass was, or even who 'Them' actually were. It was so damnable it could never have been funny, even with the black humour that often sustained them on the battlefield.

They hurried through the streets as the shrapnel known as Woolly Bears burst in white clouds above them, their round bullets pinging off the cobbles and sending up dancing sparks. It would have been beautiful if it hadn't been so deadly. They tried to get down the Rue de Dixmunde and the Rue Jansenius but these were near impassable because of the fires which singed them in their thick uniforms even at a distance. They dodged whole buildings collapsing as if they had been shot, after first hearing the wooden frames crackle and then the whole structures breaking, the windows bursting with the intense heat from within. Many of the houses had their fronts sheared off as if by a huge knife and the remaining civilians cowered in their cellars, hoping that nothing else would come their way. The streets were littered with the swollen bodies of dead horses and dead men whose mutilated remains don't bear description, and they had to negotiate huge shell craters filled with water and debris, and stinking open sewers. The famous Cloth Hall was obviously being used as a ranging mark for the German guns and its broken clock lay in a twisted mess at its base.

And worst of all were the Jack Johnsons, the high explosive shells which burst with thick black fountains of cloud that made the ground shake and their ears ring and their insides turn to peasepudding, and these seemed to follow them through the burning streets, stalking them, as if it were personal.

Norman Gladden, who served with the 11th Battalion Northumberland Fusiliers and came to Ypres a year later, commented that the Germans enjoyed complete observation over the British lines and used them as a veritable anvil, against which the British troops were to be hammered mercilessly.

In fact the German artillery was firing from charts of targets that had been made years earlier, when they had accumulated peace-time ordnance survey maps. Long before the war had started they knew what to aim for when their armies eventually arrived at Ypres: rail stations and junctions, roads and cross-roads, factories, every farm or civic building that might be used for defensive purposes, every chateau that could become a headquarters.

So during the nightmare of their arrival this new batch of the Fighting Fifth did what the old soldiers among them urged: when they got a chance, they grabbed a couple of hours sleep by the side of the road and then carried on, under increasingly heavy shell fire. At one point Geordie was able to count up to 70 heavy explosions every minute, with almost nothing from the British in reply.

When they finally got to their trenches they found them shallow, ill-prepared, poxy little things that had been dug by very poor French troops who mustn't have had much heart for the battle and certainly no desire to fight to the death for *La France Profonde*.

Off to their left, over a gap of nearly two miles, the Canadians fought off waves of German infantry at Bellewaerde. They were like pit-bulls with their teeth in someone's leg, those lads: you could poke their eyes out with a hot iron but still they wouldn't give up. Even when the gas came, they still kept firing.

And the Northumberland Fusiliers themselves were hanging on by this time at Mouse Trap Farm, constantly beating off attacks from the front and their open flanks, though the German artillery had clearly got their range.

Basically they had been left to their own devices and Brigadier Sandilands, who did his own share of the fighting and more that day with the First Battalion, later noted: "The 4th, 5th, 6th and 7th Northumberland Fusiliers Territorial Force made numerous gallant attacks toward St Julien, unsupported by artillery and in the face of devastating machine gun fire."

Despite taking appalling casualties, they held their line.

Although it wasn't realised at the time except by those at the front taking a pounding, the British Army had perhaps one tenth of the equipment and material available to the Germans. Our artillery was woefully short of ammunition and at that stage had no high explosive – only shrapnel shells. None of our return artillery fire was able to break the German wire or destroy their formidable trench systems. It was only afterwards when Sir John French went public about this deficit, breaking all officers' protocols and embarrassing the Minister of War himself, Lord Kitchener, that the public outcry forced through adequate and appropriate supplies.

In the event the onslaught here at Ypres, known as the Battle of St Julien, sort of faded out. Brigadier Sandilands, who was often as bewildered by the chaotic events around him as anyone else, felt the reason the Germans didn't break through the thin khaki line was because it had been defended so resolutely they believed they were up against a far stronger force.

It might also have been because the Germans themselves had, for the moment, run short of ammunition for their heavy guns. Had they known how close they were to a breakthrough they might have pressed their attack just a little further and the war would have been theirs to win.

As it was they held back, dug in even deeper on the higher, drier ground overlooking the whole of that area, brought up their reserves, waited for new supplies, and mused on what a dogged bunch these Geordies and their marrers in other regiments were.

When I started this project during this period of convalescence on the deliberate date of April 23rd, I raised the question as to why, after the horrific slaughter on the opening day of the Somme Offensive, the entire British Army didn't just put down their guns and go home. Now, as I start to see things through Geordie's eyes, I get at least a partial answer through the events above.

Today, with omnipresent and ever-sophisticated levels of instant and global personal communication, even the humblest soul can access knowledge and information that was unimaginable in 1915. Radio communication was so much in its infancy then that it was virtually non-existent on the battlefield. Sending information from the front line back to GHQ involved the use of runners – who often got shot – or carrier pigeons – which were likely to become feather dusters as they tried to fly back to base.

Most of the time it has been the complaint of the Poor Bloody Infantry from every regiment in every battle of every war that they are never told what is going on at higher levels of conflict.

To an extent this was deliberate policy on the part of the generals who, for the most part, kept well away from the front lines. German military intelligence thought of the British as the 'blind and deaf' army, their soldiers kept in deliberate ignorance about the make-up of their formations, the names of their leaders and military affairs as a whole. They felt that captured Tommies provided them with almost no useful information, other than giving an insight into their morale (which was usually deemed, to German dismay, as being excellent). The Germans had little need for spies to act behind the British lines because they found that if they appealed to the egos and gentlemanly instincts of the British officers they captured, they were inclined to sing like birds, without ever realising the true purpose behind the Teutonic chivalry and charm. But even the officers had little idea of what was going on above battalion level.

So if I were to ask the Northumberland Fusiliers en masse on July 2nd that first *Why didn't you all revolt?* I realise now that they would have replied with a collective **Haddaway!** that would have sounded like a minenwerfer landing in an narrow trench. Quite simply, as one small part of a murderous front nearly 20 miles long, none of them really knew how dire the situation was.

And as I noted earlier, at the end of that first day most of them thought they had given a good account of themselves. And the Germans, I would add, would have agreed. We never realised, in some sectors, how close the Fritzies were to breaking.

So there was no Big Picture for the lads during the Big Push. There was no BBC, no newspapers likely to do more than tout carefully pitched tales of British pluck. Even Rudyard Kipling who lost his adored son, played his own version of the Great Game and kept up the tone with inspiring tales of individual courage in individual trenches achieving individual glory – but in a very small area, in order to inspire his huge readership. No mention of the massed slaughter that he, with his connections, was becoming fully aware of.

The opening day of the Somme Offensive was still over a year away, but that first battle the Northumberland Fusiliers of the Territorial Force found themselves in was, in retrospect, one of the crucial moments of the war.

Ypres was only ten miles from the French border and a short drive from the all important major ports on the coast. If Ypres had fallen, the Kaiser's Army would have swept through and behind the British, Belgian and French defenders. Neutral nations such as Italy, Bulgaria, Romania and Greece, watching all this, would have been inclined to join in on the German side. The blow to French and British pride would have been colossal. Empires would fall. Ypres had to be held, no matter what the cost.

Even so, there were some in France who were inclined to argue that the German hordes should have been left to access the Channel Ports. Let them take over peacefully, with an agreement to share trade and challenge the Anglo-Saxons whose perfidy at Agincourt and burning of Joan of Arc and whose lucky victory at Waterloo they detested more than the humiliation of the Franco-Prussian War in 1870. Persuade the Germans to let them have token parliaments at, say, Brussels and Strasbourg: in a few short years the true power in Europe would lie in the cunning Gallic jockey riding and directing the willing Prussian carthorse. They could possibly devise a single currency. And as for language, well, everyone wants to speak French anyway. Within a generation, they felt, the German occupiers would be so smitten by the spirit of La France that their nations would be as One: French chic, glory and style allied with German efficiency and power. Who would dare resist them? Everyone would want to join their gang.

Dream on, Jacques. Instead, those raggle-taggle defenders at Ypres spoiled everything.

There are more Whys to be answered later, most of them completely overturning my original prejudices, assumptions and bigotry about all sorts of things. But let's look more closely at the Geordies' daily life within the trenches now that we've got them there.

The Northumberland Fusiliers were not constantly in one sector, fighting the same endless battles in the same place. The battalions were rotated between 'quiet' and very active sectors, in order to maintain some degree of freshness. This was one advantage they had over their opponents who didn't rotate in the same way and were often disconcerted to find, when they themselves were near exhausted, they were suddenly faced with fresh troops who had increasing levels of equipment and preparation.

So what would our avatar do when he wasn't being bombed and shot at, and not being made to go charging up that hill with bayonet fixed and getting stuck in the wire which – yet again – hadn't been destroyed even after days of bombardment?

Depending on the season he would get up before dawn at, say 4 a.m., and this was known as:

Stand To. He would be ready for immediate action, with bayonet fixed, gas mask to hand and Mills Bombs at the ready. The snipers would move silently into position and the look-outs would scan No Man's Land with their periscopes for any sign of an impending attack. This would be followed at about 5 a.m. by:

Inspection. In which platoon and company commanders would check the state of the men and their equipment and also the state of their feet. And if you think that's an over-reaction then try googling images of Trench Foot but be prepared to throw up. Then they would clean their rifles. After inspection would be:

Breakfast. Hot tea and stew would be brought along the trench from the distant cookhouse in flat, barrel-like containers with screw-down lids which were strapped over the orderly's shoulders. Sometimes they just got tins of cold meat and vegetables called Maconochies, after the maker. Sometimes a shot of rum also. Then would come:

Fatigues. Which involved more digging, filling sandbags for building traverses or adding to the breastworks, doing all those chores necessary to keep themselves in good fighting trim and their trenches habitable, while never once poking their heads above the parapet. Then they spent time:

Chatting. This was not a case of the Geordies 'cracking away' among themselves, which was (is) their term for animated conversation, but time spent trying to remove the omnipresent lice from the seams of their uniforms[60]. During this time also they might write letters home, read, play cards, moan, kill as many rats as they could, speculate, clean their rifles again and then have more fatigues then finally the moment known as:

Stand Down, which was just before dusk, in which every man had to be ready for final attack of the day.

Then they would crawl into their little shelters built into the sides of the trenches, where possible, praying the gas alarm wouldn't sound, hoping the shelling might lessen or even stop, hearing the rising and falling crescendos of distant machine guns and rifles which never quite ceased and told stories of other people's troubles. Often they were all so close they could even hear the Alleyman voices coming to them across No Man's Land, where occasionally the Captain would ask for volunteers to go on patrol. Surprisingly, a few did, because some felt it was safer out there, at night, than anywhere else in daylight. As long as they froze into bizarre positions when the flares were sent up they would stand a good chance of doing something useful, like repairing their own wire, or inspecting the enemy wire before a future attack.

But they had to gan canny because the Germans were so windy they kept sending up their Very Lights every five minutes, so frequently that the British were able to conserve their own limited supplies. And most of all they tried to sleep, and dream of good things at home, and their next leave.

Which in itself was a problem for the Geordies.

Although the officers had a comparatively generous leave allowance, the privates' passes were usually only for 5 days, and then only depending on manpower available. After the pounding they had had at St Julien their commanding officer couldn't have had much leeway when it came to granting it. Besides, the catch was that a pass for 5 days leave had to include travel time. Men from the regiments in Kent, for example, could get home in a day if they were very lucky. But by the time a Geordie got back to Tyneside from Flanders he had to come straight back. And if he was late he would be done for going AWOL.

---

60 I see that the Irish word 'craic' is in common usage now but we were not aware of that spelling. It was always 'cracking away' or 'having a good crack' and there were no sexual or narcotic connotations.

Many wretches went a couple of years before they saw their families again. And then they hadn't a clue what to talk to them about, because how could you describe seeing your best mate's face torn off by shrapnel, or watching men with no limbs bleeding to death and screaming for their mams, or having your corporal's brains spread all over your jacket like jam?

How could he even talk about the simpler things, like having to spend days in the disgusting stink of a shallow trench filled with shit because it was impossible to get out during daylight, and trying to get through mud so deep that horses and heavily-kitted soldiers would get sucked down and drown? Or about the terror of looking up, almost vertically, at the lighted tail of a minenwerfer bomb turning over and over as it began to fall, and wondering if you could get away in time while it came toward you with a noise like an express train. Or the way that the ground was constantly shaking from the artillery of both sides and that somewhere, always, there were men in pain in the darkness calling for help. How could Wor Geordie explain to Jinny and his young bairns Elsie and Little Geordie, who were just beginning to talk, what Hell was like?

Away from the front line however, it was possible to have a spurious sense of normality in the little villages that were well behind the German shelling.

Geordie would have spent odd days at the delightful Poperinghe where he would find something of the continental experience he might have hoped for. At very least he and the lads could get properly clean, either by being blasted with a two inch hosepipe or a communal warm bath in one of the converted vats of the local brewery, making all the expected jokes about piss and foreign beer, while attempts were made in a laundry to steam clean the lice from their uniforms. There were shops, stalls which sold fruit, a small library run by the YMCA, cafés and restaurants where they could get their all-time favourite of egg and chips – and much else besides.

Or they could go to Reninghelst where for once the men were in good huts and the officers – for some reason – in tents, and they could enjoy the Divisional Concert Party known as 'The Fancies', starring those two famous beauties Miss Lanoline and

Miss Marjorine who had them in stitches, though not all of the lads realised they weren't really women they were baying at. Music at these places was provided by the former regimental bandsmen whose instruments were not much use on the Western Front and so they became stretcher bearers instead – one of the most onerous roles of all. But they really let rip with their tubas on these occasions and at times like this you could almost forget there was a war on.

And when King George and HRH the Prince of Wales visited their areas of woe and destruction with their Colonel Wilkinson, and came right up to the front line, the lads admired them enormously, and there was none of this Why nonsense from them that you're getting from me.

But the Germans weren't going to just get up and go away; the battles never really stopped. Historians talk about the First, Second and Third Battles of Ypres but for those who were there it started in August 1914 and never really stopped until November 1918, and was far worse than Verdun.

We are so used to watching violence on the television screens that we tend to see it all as compacted into one small area of our consciousness, carefully timed to finish before the News at Ten. Or, if it's really violent, only starting after the watershed of 9 p.m. The warfare in France and Flanders went on and on and – quite literally – bloody on. No matter which channel you tuned into, or which part of the Front, you could be seeing the same thing and not know where you are or when you are within the history of the real war.

One of the most disturbing things I've found in reading about the battles is that they all seemed inconclusive. From the first day of the Somme Offensive to the last, it was the same tactic, the same barrage, the same preparation, the same nightmare slaughter and the same (apparent) non-result.

One sergeant asked his major despairingly why they kept making the same old attacks in winter when they were always going to fail, but the officer, his face a mask of sorrow, could only shrug. He was doing his best, and at his level it wasn't his role to ask questions.

Modern historians have considerably revised the stereotypical notion of the Lions led by Donkeys that is by now ingrained in us.

They argue that when looked at in broader context, also taking into account German perceptions of these battles, the British leadership was actually highly professional and effective. As I read more and more, wider and deeper, I can find as many accounts of the men at the Front who would agree with this as I can the opposite.

I come to see that we all recreate the history of the War as we might devise our own perceptions of our family. My sister reading all this about our Dad might well be able to make no connection with the man I knew, and I'm rather afraid to show this book to her. When I first met my Uncle Jack, Dad's youngest brother, I asked him about our grandfather, the War Hero, but he had no memories of him at all, except as a quiet presence in the back room who didn't say much. On the other hand he told me all about my Dad's vast assortment of birds' eggs that he had collected and itemised and labelled as a boy, roaming far and wide over the fields around the town.

"I didn't know that," I had to confess. "I didn't see that side of him at all, and he never mentioned it." I went quiet. Sometimes, that's the safest and perhaps only option when you get stuck in a trench of your own perceptions and prejudices.

So I begin to see that when we dive into the collective morass of the War Experience and grab what seems to be familiar or perhaps comforting, we can get startled. We might grab a hand reaching out to us from the mud and find there is only an arm and no body attached. We might rescue a compatriot from the darkness of No Man's Land and find it is an enemy you have spent weeks shooting at.

I start to suspect that General Douglas Haig did the very best he could, with unseen and usually unacknowledged flair, and that men like my grandfather saw that and adored him for it.

But my god that makes me uncomfortable after the decades of scorn and prejudice that I've thrown in his direction.

No letters from Geordie back home to Ashington have survived to tell us what he was going through, though he would certainly have written many. Nor have any from Jinny to her brave husband in the trenches come to light. In the latter case, very few letters from any family to the men serving on the Western Front have come down to posterity quite simply because they were likely to have been used as toilet paper. Only officers had a supply of the latter. The men used what they could.

Again, the ex-miners among the Northumberland Fusiliers would have done as they did down the pits – used their hands. This is where the Geordie term 'winnit' came from. The word itself means 'will not', but in this context the 'winnits' were the lumps of faecal matter stuck to the hair around the anus that winnit come off.

The War Diary of the 6th Battalion hasn't survived, presumably because they took such a battering that they had to blend in with the 4th, whose partial diary did survive. We can look at this to get a general sense of events.[61]

War Diary for Sanctuary Wood. 12 – 24 Feb 1916

12th Feb 1916

That night the Bn relieved the 9th Bn DLI[62] in the Sanctuary Wood trenches. Relief went quite quietly. At 8am on the 13th the enemy began shelling Hooge Ridge, just to the left of the Bn. The bombardment continued all day with the Germans firing an estimated six thousand shells. Sanctuary Wood was on the receiving end of some of them and a few fusiliers from the 4th Bn wounded. The night passed off fairly quietly. During the morning of the 14th there was only little activity. In the afternoon the enemy shelled Hooge Ridge again and late in the afternoon attacked opposite the Rifle Bde positions but were beaten back. A good amount of stuff was thrown over the 4th Bn trenches, killing four men and wounding about 13 or 14. On the right flank, opposite the 17th Divn, the enemy in the afternoon bombarded very heavily and attacked taking a few of our trenches. Our Bn transport was shelled while returning through Kruisstraat, one Cpl was killed and two men wounded. Just before 3.30pm on the 14th the enemy opened up with a heavy bombardment on the Hooge trenches, held by the 24th Divn, on the immediate left flank of the 50th Divn. At 3.30pm shelling of trenches 37, 38 and 39 (opposite Hill 60 and astride the railway) and the area to the rear held by the 150th Bde. The 149th Bde had the 7th Bn on the right and the 4th on the left, the 6th Bn in close support and the 5th in Bde reserve. The 149th Bde, however, seem to escape the very

---

61 Extracted from the excellent website: http://www.4thbnnf.com/index.html
 All attempts to contact the creator of this site have come to nothing.
62 Durham Light Infantry

heavy bombardment to which units on their right and left were subjected; The whole of the day the trenches immediately to our right and left came in for a very heavy and, at times, intense bombardment, and it was apparent that the enemy intended to put in an attack at some point or other. All the approaches up from Kruistraat were shelled with 'whizz-bangs'[63] and HE,[64] and the Bde Office at Zillebeke dugouts was blown in and a good deal of material destroyed. The bombardment continued until 5pm.

15th Feb 1916

The night was disturbed and at 4.30am a counterattack was made on the lost trenches but failed. The whole of the day was rather disturbed; the enemy shelled Hooge Ridge and round about, but nothing further happened. On the 14th there was an attack on the left flank, during which some of the enemy's bombers were opposite our trenches, but they were spotted and dispersed. During the night two rifles, two grenades and the belongings of one of them who was shot were safely recovered to the trenches. The information gained turned out to be of great value to GHQ. At 8pm another counterattack was made on the lost trenches and met with partial success.

16th Feb 1916

The whole of the day was quiet on both sides. In the evening the Bn was relieved from the front line and moved into close support redoubts. HQ went to Maple Copse. Capt J.R. Robb and 2nd Lt Scaife returned from leave and no officers being due, all leave went to men.

17th – 20th Feb Maple Copse

Nothing much to record during these four days. The Bn supplied seven working parties each night and lay in support during the daytime. On the night of the 20th we came up to trenches again and took over. Owing to the low strength of the Bn, the 7th Bn take control of the right hand trench, relieving the pressure greatly.

In trenches at Sanctuary Wood. A good deal of snow on the ground, but artillery less active on both sides.

---

63 Popular slang name for a high velocity German artillery shell. Describes the sound it made passing through the air and on explosion.
64 High Explosive

22nd – 24th Feb 1916

All these three days passed quietly, and there were no casualties.

There are matter-of-fact comments made by that young officer which are heart-breaking:

A good amount of stuff was thrown over the trenches
A counter attack was made on the lost trenches and failed
Another counterattack was made on the lost trenches and met with partial success
The night passed off fairly quietly.

Behind those laconic comments lay levels of violence and horror that most people will never know in their entire lives. This young lad just had to get on with it: do his fighting, set a good example, keep up with all the reports – and try to look after his men as if he were their dad.

The very names, Maple Copse and Sanctuary Wood… they sound as if they could have been sylvan places down at the River Wansbeck near Ashington, or else the idyllic parkland known as Jesmond Dene in the heart of Newcastle. But these were places of true evil and in reality the only trees left were mere spelks above the torn and shattered ground, not a leaf remaining, what was left of the ground covered in an area of stinking, rotting flesh that had once been human beings and which were now unrecognisable bits that the rats and crows were gorging on.

And then there was Thiepval, where a large portion of what had been the Newcastle United first team went into battle for the first time.

Before the war Newcastle had started to buy talented players, especially from Scotland, and soon had a squad to rival all of England. With players like Colin Veitch, Jackie Rutherford, Jimmy Lawrence and Albert Shepherd, the Magpies soon had a team of international talent. There were local players such as Bill

McCracken, Jimmy Howie, Peter McWilliam and Andy Aitken who were household names. They lifted the League Championship on three occasions and reached five FA Cup finals in the years leading up to 1914 and Geordie fans had enjoyed ten years of being the team everyone wanted to topple. They played a style of possession football that was entertaining and rousing.

These lads were heroes on Tyneside before they ever put on a uniform. They had a right winger who could catch racing pigeons and who gave his opposing full back twisted blood as he cruised past and got in a cross. They had a centre half who would approach any rookies against him and threaten to snap their backs if they dared to come near, and so *gliffed the witch oot o' them*[65] before the game even started. The centre forward, wearing the legendary number 9, was so grizzly strong he had three men marking him even at the warm-up, and no-one could head the heavy ball like he could. And then they had two brilliantly nasty full backs who would tackle so hard and in such a way that the wingers trying to get past would be sent sprawling over the cinder track which ran around the pitch, scraping the skin off their legs.

They were professionals, this lot. Naturally fit, genuinely hard, with a never-say-die attitude. They learned their lessons during army training fast and they learned them well. They were role models, determined to inspire the rest of the lads as much here in Belgium as they ever had in the football grounds up and down the country. They had trained hard and now they wanted to fight easy, so they could get back home and do what they did best.

The recommended assault tactics this battalion used for going over the top were – as ever – devised by senior Staff Officers who had a reputation for never going near the front line. The manuals of the time specified that battalions should advance in waves with two platoons per wave on a 400-yard front – which left about 5 yards between each soldier. A battalion would therefore advance in eight waves (two per company) plus additional waves for the battalion HQ and stretcher bearers. The advance would be carried out at a steady walking pace of 50 yards per minute.

Soldiers in the leading waves were required to carry about 70lb of equipment; rifle, bayonet, ammunition, two grenades, entrenching tool, empty sandbags, wire cutters, flares, etc. The later waves would also be burdened with the necessary paraphernalia for

---

[65] Inspire sudden terror.

consolidating the captured trenches such as ladders, bombs, barbed wire and stakes.

In essence, the Northumberland Fusiliers were told before the battle the preliminary artillery barrage would be so intense that they should be able to approach with walking sticks in place of rifles, and that there was no need to run. Just in case though, they should attack in 'true Northumbrian fashion', with fixed bayonets, and they mustn't worry about the machine guns because there wouldn't be any left by the time the artillery wallahs had finished.

When the whistle blew to go over the top the troops gave a great roar as they had done for their heroes so many times before at St James' Park, and Corporal Dunglinson and Private Goodwill both kicked footballs toward the German lines, while the latter tried a bit of keepy-up as he advanced.

The Germans watched all this with some degree of horror. They were relatively new troops themselves from the 99th Regiment, and when they saw those large brown round objects being kicked toward them they assumed them to be a new kind of bomb.

As the Fusiliers advanced they all thought that, for once, the officers had got it right because there was no immediate firing from the German lines. Although it was a bit worrying that their barbed wire seemed intact. Still, just one last boot with the ball and –

The Germans opened fire. They fired with machine-guns and rifles. They used rifle grenades and lobbed stick grenades. The British artillery barrage had been so ineffective that the Germans came out of their trenches, stood upon their parapets and waved to our men to come on, jeering at them, and picked them off at leisure. They fired until their guns got almost too hot to hold. Still the Geordies came on. As one of the German defenders noted:

> The British continued to advance against the 5th Company and the right wing of the 6th, protected by the remains of the trees of the little wood which used to stand in front of their trenches. Men of the two companies threw themselves against the enemy with a thunderous cheer, and there ensued a wild hand-to-hand combat.[66]

No-one could withstand that. The Fusiliers' advance was checked and the waves of attackers, or what was left of them, were forced

---

[66] From report by Albrecht Stosch, written in 1927. Quoted in *Through German Eyes* by Christopher Duffy.

to lie down. And then, finally, crawl back to their own trenches to 'stand fast' and hold the line.

They went through hell, Alan. Ah wish Ah'd acknowledged that in me Dad. He tried tae tell iz once or twice but ah deliberately didn't lissen. Divvn't ask why. He went through hell.
But so did you go through hell.
Eh? Not like that son.
No, no... but you suffered more undeserved pain, madness, cruelty and mind games than I've seen in any relationship since, but you came through.
Aye weel, Ah had tae. Ye couldn't just divorce then. What would hae become of you and Pat? Ah had tae stay, Ah had tae stick it.
Dad, amid all the stories I'm reading and telling about these heroes of a different kind, you showed as much courage, dignity and endurance as any of them.
Did Ah? Ah did me best.
You held the line Dad. You held it.
Haddaway...

At least The Northumberland Fusiliers had a notable victory at St Eloi in April 1916.

They'd been fighting there since 1915 without making any progress. It was the worst of the trench war battlefields with poorly prepared British trenches facing well prepared positions of the opposing side, a mere 100 yards apart. The British trenches were formed into three sets: the forward fire trench that was nearly waist deep in water; the rear trench about 2 feet under water; the 'extension trench' was a staggering 5 feet deep, with the bottom of each trench covered in a clinging mud of a sort you would never get in England; this stuff was glutinous, sticky and would suck you down. It has been estimated that thousands of horses and heavily laden men drowned in the stuff.

Trench duty meant that they were trapped in the water because if they moved during daylight they would get shot by the excellent snipers firing from the enemy line. Because the trench was so narrow it was even difficult to move within it without creating a wave of water, mud and shit that would further upset everybody around. Nowhere to sit, nowhere to lie, not even a place to keep your rifle in the dry for the whole 48 hours of duty.

This then was the temporary 'home' for the Northumberland Fusiliers when on trench duty, but the discomfort wasn't limited to standing in what was virtually a sewer. Empty rations tins were used to scoop out the shit and piss, then having been used they were slung forward from the trench into No Man's Land. A diary of the time recorded: "It was purgatory for me ... I had diarrhoea 14 times during daylight ... I was in a dreadful state when I eventually got to the hospital".

Somehow, despite all that, they captured the German lines, at least for a little while.

Their exultation when they did win is evident in the official photograph which was turned into a postcard for the troops to send home, and was widely circulated in magazines. *The Graphic* used this for its full cover, with the banner headline trumpeting: THE 'FIGHTING FIFTH' IN THEIR GLORY. A BATTLEFIELD PICTURE FROM ST. ELOI.[67] We see the triumphant Tommies cheering and posing for the camera, some of them dressed up in captured German headgear, and many of them waving their defeated foes' weapons.

67 *The Graphic*. April 29th 1916.

I had stumbled upon this when, during a restless night, I felt compelled to get up at 3 a.m. and google for more images about World War 1. I found this particular one on *Amazon*, someone offering for sale the front and back pages of the original magazine, which I promptly bought via that one-click ordering method which might eventually bankrupt me, then went back to bed.

Yet there was something very odd about this picture. It bothered me hugely like the *pit lie idle, pit lie idle* refrain that had stuck in my mind like an ear-worm, as the Germans term it. As before when the Northumberland Fusiliers started marching in my head and kept me from sleep I got up again and found the link, determined to do a screen capture of the image before the original arrived.

The *Amazon* page enabled me to scan across the item and zoom in with extraordinary clarity, so it was like being pulled into the Looking Glass: There were boys who probably should have been at school. Grizzled soldiers posing with weapons. Satisfied and relieved-looking officers and their NCOs. Hard lads posing with their captured Jarmin headgear and having a 'tab', as the Geordies called their cigarettes...

I remembered what Dad had said once about how – as Wor Geordie told his son on a rare occasion when they *were* talking – a 'Prussian' had nearly got him. I had always assumed that he was using the term Prussian in the generic sense, as referring to *any* German. Yet the headgear they're flaunting are not the metal ones with the familiar spikes, but instead the sort known as 'shakos', bearing the emblems of the elite Prussian *Jägerbataillon*.

The government would have quite happy to splash these pictures for the nation: young lads at home would see what fun they were apparently having out in Flanders and decide they wanted some of that action too. But most startling of all, as I zoomed in further, I saw this fella waving his tin hat and the hair on my neck stood on end...

That was him, my grandad, the Geordie of Geordies. As I sat on a creaky computer chair in my little flat in the heart of Wiltshire, almost a hundred years after this was taken in a Flanders field, there he was sitting on the ground and waving right at me...

Haddaway son. Hoo d'ye knaa that?
I do Dad, **I know** it.
Aye whey, but he was a grey haired old man when Ah knew him best.
We all get like that Dad. 'Whither the Fates Goest' as the motto said.
Divvn't get smart Alan, it doesn't suit ye.

10

GIVING A PUSH

THE BATTLES went on. And on. The slaughter unrelenting, war without end. Wor Geordie was in the thick of it although it is known that he was 'Sick to Hospital' in December 1915, just before and probably during Christmas. What was wrong? It could have been dysentery which was very common and had a diabolical effect; it could have been frostbite, Trench Foot, various kinds of gas poisoning or something he picked up from the omnipresent rats. It could have been influenza, bronchitis, pneumonia, shell shock, venereal disease or even self-inflicted injury. It was estimated that over 90,000 men died during the Great War from non-military causes.

But when he came back to his battalion in early 1916 everyone soon became aware that something nameless, very secret and very important was being planned that could, if it worked, end the war.

This was the Big Push. The level of preparation for which was incredible.

They couldn't do anything about the mud but they supplied pumps that would, they hoped, drain at least some of the water from under the duckboards of the trenches.

More pumping equipment was brought from Britain to provide water for drinking, washing and laundry. 300 large lorries with 550 gallon tanks brought water to the billets so that they didn't have to rely too much on chlorinating existing supplies.

They couldn't do anything about the natural height advantage the German lines enjoyed but they introduced Observation Balloons whose pilots passed information down via the use of flags or occasionally by radio. The operators would generally remain in the air for hours at a spell, and there were very few men who would swap their place in the trenches for their job up in the air.

200,000 men were made available. To keep them fit during the long weeks before the Big Push began, they were given regular inspections of kit, gas masks, rations, rifles, feet, genitals, eyes and all other body parts whose impaired efficiency might have a detrimental effect when it came to fighting.

They were given route marches, ferocious levels of physical training, lectures, weapons drill, bathing parades and laundry parades. They practised their rifle skills to get them up to the level of skill shown by the average *landser*.

The Royal Engineers laid 43,000 miles of cables above ground so that HQ could communicate with the front lines. Just in case these got damaged by shelling, they also buried another 7000 miles of telephone cables deep underground.

If the electronic signals failed, the Carrier Pigeon Service prepared 150 mobile lofts for use by 22,000 pigeons.

Working at night and in deep secrecy, with as much silence as possible, they created hidden locations from which their heavy artillery could fire on the enemy and a system of coloured flares and klaxons were developed for use whereby the Royal Flying Corps could communicate with the ground troops – particularly artillery.

Various riflemen had shining metal disks sewn on the back of their uniforms to enable the artillery observers to judge how far away they were, and so lay down an accurate barrage on their behalf, and avoid any possibility of friendly fire casualties.

There were soldiers specially trained to use long explosive 'torpedoes' which would remove any fragments of wire which did survive. And others who would carry ladders that would enable the attackers to cross the enemy trenches with ease.

To supply the big guns the sappers created nearly 100 miles of standard gauge railway track that would ferry ammunition to new-built railheads all along the front.

Engineers also built large models of the German defences, exactly to scale, with all the trenches, pill boxes and fortified houses in miniature, so that the soldiers would have a clearer idea of what they were up against, rather than lines on a map.

Eleven casualty stations were set up along 16 miles of front and the quality of the immediate roads were improved to cope with the increase of heavy transport. This time, no vehicles were going to get stuck in the mud on their way to do battle or give succour. Tunnels were constantly being dug with great skill, often by ex-miners, deep into enemy lines and below their defences, primed with huge quantities of explosive which would be set off at the agreed moment.

They built and supplied fleets of ambulances, dozens of dressing stations and even had a few pre-prepared cemeteries for the low casualties expected.

Any development, any technique likely to improve the accuracy of the shelling was considered, practised and developed far away from the front, so that it would all come as a horrible surprise to the Germans when hell was unleashed upon them.

And still it all went disastrously wrong.

Yet if you were one of the 20 million people who watched the film *The Battle of the Somme*, which was the first documentary of its kind, you would have come away thinking we had achieved something magnificent, despite the cost in men. Which no-one *really* knew about at the time.

As I said earlier, trying to get some sense of it, every word in this book represented one death or serious injury for that first day alone. By the time the whole Somme Offensive faded out 5 months later in November then you have to think in terms of every *letter* of this book as representing a body.

The British daily loss rate during the ongoing Battle of the Somme was 2,943 men.[68] All in all the British and French armies gained about six miles by the end of the Offensive. Every inch of ground cost four men. British casualties for that period came to 419,654. French casualties were 202,567. The German casualties were conservatively estimated at 465,181.

I think that since those dread events beginning July 1st 1916 we've all tended to assume that the Battle of the Somme was a complete disaster, but later historians, perhaps more in tune with the ordinary Tommy and Poilu, have argued that it was actually an Allied victory. As British historian Gary Sheffield said, "The battle of the Somme was not a victory in itself, but without it the Entente would not have emerged victorious in 1918".

But why didn't all go according to General Haig's meticulous plan? Why was there no sweeping breakthrough?

---

68 Which exceeded the loss rate during the Third Battle of Ypres but was not as severe as the two months of the Battle of Arras (4,076 per day) or the final Hundred Days offensive in 1918 (3,685 per day).

Quite simply the explosives failed to break the wire despite five days of continuous bombardment. The Germans were dug in so deeply in their bomb-proof bunkers that, although they themselves suffered huge casualties, there was still enough of them to come out and man their machine gun posts when the shelling stopped.

Wire and machine guns stopped them.

A lot of the senior officers blamed the fact that one shell in five failed to explode, and serious questions were asked about the workers at Armstrong's factory and similar places, although most people recognised this was a case of the servants getting the blame when the upper classes get themselves into trouble.

Norman Gladden, who first joined the 7th Bn Northumberland Fusiliers (Territorial Force) and hated their parochialism, but adored his fellow soldiers in the 11th Bn, fought in the Somme and later in the equally dreadful Third Battle of Ypres. Despite all the preparations for the former he had no clear idea in his mind of anything purposeful happening there, but was deeply impressed by what he saw being done at the latter. He thought that the build-up of the Big Push was taken to an even higher level at Ypres, where he felt that he was involved in something momentous, world-changing, as some would later confess to feeling during the build up to the Normandy Invasion of 1944.

And despite the slaughter of both he later reflected:

> At times I, who was so young... felt tired, forlorn and cut off from all the people and things I cared for, immured in a sort of evil cell that was but the antechamber to death. It was only from the feeling that we were with those who were doing their duty and that we were suffering for those whom we had left behind, and for the ideals and future of our country, that any real consolation could be derived.

Knowing what I know now, how would I answer if the spirit of General Douglas Haig were to come through to me at a Psychic Fayre in Glastonbury and say to me in that abrupt way he had, without the slightest word of apology:

Well... what would you have done sonny?

I would not have an adequate reply. As a desk-bound and somewhat private Individual who has not the slightest experience of what individual Privates went through on the battlefield, I would have no wise or clever insight to give him. I can't see what more the General Head Quarters planners could have done for the lads.

So what should the soldiers themselves have done? Fling down their rifles and go home? It never entered their heads.[69]

Which more or less answers my original question.

On the 22nd June 1917 Private George Matthew Richardson managed to get some worthwhile leave in Ashington. He had an important meeting at the Town Hall but had just downed a quick pint in his old haunt and second home of the Grand Hotel. He lit up a tab and stood outside the door, staring north to the pit heaps and thinking how this looked just like the area around Loos had done before the shelling started.

Jinny had wanted to come with him because people of their class never got a chance to go to such a posh place but he had to do this alone. Besides, it was very awkward between them, in the personal sense, and he spent all his time playing with the bairns to hide the fact that he didn't know what to say to her. He was a different man these days to the young barman who had left. He wasn't afraid of her dad any more, and in fact John Yellowley had looked at him with gratifying respect and slipped a ten shilling note into his top pocket with a firm *Ssh!*

Slightly nervous about the next half hour, he took deep breaths and hoped Jinny would be proud of him after this. He could handle rifles, blast away with Lewis Guns and hoy 'toffee apples' with the best of them, but the idea that he would have to give some sort of speech was nerve-wracking.

He was joined by Petty Officer Tom Egdell, a lad who had come into the Grand a few times before the war, but other than pulling him a pint they hadn't had much to talk about. Now, in the same situation, they had a million shells, oceans of mud and thousands of bodies in foreign fields in common. Although Geordie couldn't think of anything to say to Jinny and felt they were worlds apart, Tom and him didn't need to say a word to each other but felt oddly close.

---

69 Old soldiers after the Great War insisted it was a myth that MPs were on hand to shoot anyone who didn't go over the top.

They marched together, in step, to the Town Hall, and both wondered if the one at Ypres had once looked like this. They couldn't get over how quiet the town was, compared to where they had just spent the past few years.

They were met at the door by Councillor W.S. Pattison, who greeted them both on behalf of the Ashington and District Distinguished Service Recognition Society, and were given hearty hand-shakes by Mr. B. Walker, Miss Williams, and Mr. G. Beaty who was the Hon. Sec. of the society.

They were both there to be presented with a gold Hunter watch, suitably inscribed. These were not cheap devices. They were Waltham Watches, made by the Illinois Watch Case Co. from Elgin U.S.A. and guaranteed to be made of two plates of gold, with a Plate of Composition, and would wear for 20 years. Although expensive, the two men there deserved no less.

Petty Officer Egdell, the Councillor explained, had been awarded the Distinguished Conduct Medal for conspicuous bravery and constant devotion to duty. On one occasion he had advanced over the open ground single-handed, and with a Lewis gun he was able to save a large portion of his division being cut off by the enemy. He had fought in Antwerp, the Dardanelles, and France.[70]

Private Richardson, he went on to add, had been awarded the Military Medal for removing wounded men to safety while under heavy fire, and for rescuing two sergeants from a dug-out which had been blown in by a high explosive shell, and in addition to the Military Medal with Bar had also been recommended for the Distinguished Conduct Medal.

The Councillor then spoke in admiring terms of the great bravery of the men who had gone from the Ashington district and the valuable work they had done both on land and sea. They were living, he said, in an age when honour should be given where due. It would have been very discreditable and unpatriotic of the public of Ashington to allow Petty Officer Egdell and Private Richardson

---

70 KX/490 Petty Officer Thomas Egdell, Hood Bn. Royal Naval Volunteer Reserve. Died of Wounds 24th September 1917 aged 37. Born Alnwick, Northumberland 25/11/1879. A Miner. Wife, Alice, 277 Maple St., Ashington, Northumberland. Awarded Distinguished Conduct Medal (in action at Grandcourt 3-5/2/17) London Gazette 26/3/17 : "For conspicuous gallantry in action. He got his machine guns into action under heavy fire & greatly assisted in repelling a strong enemy counter-attack. He set a fine example of courage & initiative."

to visit their homes and not to have shown some appreciation of their services to humanity and the honours they had gained on the field of battle. He hoped the war would soon be over, and that both the recipients would accept the watches as a kind of token of the goodwill of the public towards them and that the watches would ever remind them of their duty well done.

His words come across almost reproachfully. This was not directed at the two heroes but clearly toward some people in the committee who had not been happy about spending so much money, on these two watches, for these two lads. Councillor Pattison was probably an old soldier himself, who would have felt that those particular duffers would have made good Staff Officers for the way they hadn't a clue about the real things in life, tight buggers that they were.

And then, as the local newspaper the *Morpeth Herald* reported:

> Both recipients suitably replied and thanked the committee for their kind thought. Votes of thanks brought another of these many and interesting gatherings to a close.

"Let's hev a pint," said the relieved Geordie afterward, looking at the time on his brand new watch to see if the Grand was still open. But every moment he was there, like all the Tommies, he would have a lurking sense of 'letting the side down', of being safe at home while his mates were sticking it out and he wasn't with them, sharing the hard work, the terror and the mud. Him and young Edgell would have hated it at the Front and yet wanted to go straight back, because they'd feel that anywhere else was shirking, and Flanders had become their one reality.

Mind you, things couldn't have been too strained between him and Jinny: they must have had some fun between the sheets during his brief period of leave because his second son, William Haig Richardson, was born 9 months later.

It was Dad's Watch which told me all this because it gave the date of the presentation. I felt sure that even if all the Army records had long been lost, the local newspapers of the time would have made some mention of it. The archivists at the admirable County

Records Office, now based in the old Woodhorn Colliery where both Georges' briefly worked, came up trumps.

Almost at the same time I had an email from Graham Stewart, co-author of the excellent tome *Tyneside Scottish*, who seems to lurk behind various on-line military forums like some eminence grise, with what appears to be a total knowledge of the Great War in general and the Northumberland Fusiliers in particular.

His brief paragraph enabled me to give Wor Geordie some sort of actual, rather than virtual, placing within the events of the time. How he was able to do this from the middle of Saudi Arabia is something I find bewilderingly marvellous. I wonder if I should put him in touch with those lassies from St Petersburg who still pop up when I'm on-line?[71]

> Pte George Matthew Richardson – resident of Ashington, Northumberland. Enlisted into the 6th Bn, 29th June 1915. Was "Sick to Hospital" 15th December 1915 and known to have been wounded on the 25th & 26th May 1916 – probably the reason why he was transferred to the 13th Bn on recovery. On his transfer to the 13th Bn he was renumbered '37829' and recorded as wounded again in May 1918

He also pointed out also that the uniform grandad was wearing was his SD (Service Dress) jacket and the little blurry badge on the left breast pocket was the Military Medal ribbon with the 'Silver Rosette' sewn to it, which indicates 'the Bar'. I had wondered what that was.

His information was quite startling, and helped give a 3D quality to grandad's photograph. I had assumed that this had been taken when he first joined up, his fresh and cheeky face full of hope and enthusiasm, with no sense of the terrors which would come. In fact when the watch had been presented on the 22nd of June the medal badge showed he had already won the M.M. and Bar and been in the war for years. This was not a rookie I was looking at but an Old Soldier, and the photograph may well have been taken for the presentation.

Graham's information was crucial. He apologised for being geeky but as far as I'm concerned, in these situations where I've found myself floundering, the geeks can inherit the earth.

---

71 They're very kind. They're so impressed by my on-line research into Trench Foot that they've offered to put a large sum of money into my bank account.

GIVING A PUSH

Like the stories that Uncle Jack told me about my Dad which caused me to change my perceptions and 'see' him on my little cinema screen in a completely different way, this observation by Graham made me look at Grandfather Geordie afresh. He also gave me the dates of when he had been Gazetted.

Eh? I thought, when I saw the term for the first time.

Being Gazetted, as I came to learn, meant that the award had become official when published in the *St George's Gazette* or *The Times* – although they even mentioned him in Edinburgh too. No promotion or award was generally regarded as 'official' until it had been gazetted.

GAZETTED:

4214	11th OCTOBER	1916	[PRESENTED MM]
37829	11th MAY	1917	[PRESENTED MM]
37829	28th JULY	1917	DELETED

No further details are given in these gazettes as far as I can find, just dates. The date of the 28th July 'Deleted' must refer to his nomination for the DCM which, somehow, was not ultimately approved. I have not the slightest idea what circumstances might be involved here. In those days, only the deeds of the officer class were detailed.

At this too, along with Graham's crucial emails, I got a package of information from the Fusiliers Museum at Alnwick, which showed that they had been as bewildered by the different Medal Cards and regimental numbers as myself. Not only did two of the cards show him as having two different numbers (4214 and 37829) referring to the 6th and 13th Battalions respectively, but there was a third (undated) card for G.M. Richardson 4214 who went to France on the 11th November 1915 but served with the Royal Flying Corps!

In writing biographies of other, deliberately private individuals, I became wary of those labyrinths of biographical detail and mystery which have led me, twisting and turning, following the spoor toward the centre where all the noise seemed to be coming from, only to find a very dead Red Herring. G.M. Richardson of the RFC could not have been Wor Geordie.

The researchers of the Fusilier Museum determined that our man, my grandad, would have fought in the battlegrounds around Albert, Mametz and Millencourt when he was with the 6th. Later, with the 13th Battalion, the fighting would have been in the area of Boyells, the Sensee River, Fontaine-les-Croisilles and Moyenville. They also saw that he had been wounded in the 'Winnipeg' trench system near Kemmel by artillery activity on May 25th 1916, and then a victim again, but more seriously this time, on May 26th when he got hit by trench mortar fire.

When you read of tragic parents who have lost children, had them snatched or just can't face up to the fact of their deaths, they look for them in every crowd. In a small way I do this with my grandad, scanning every anecdote, every yarn every anonymous incident and wonder if I can find him or fit him into the story in order to make sense of my needs and hopes.

Norman Gladden who would have seen or perhaps known him in both battalions wrote about a jolly pay parade in a camp well away from the front line. The canteen was well stocked with beer, everyone seemed to be singing the Blaydon Races, and there were numerous brawls. A few of the younger lads, tanked up, made a dead set at what he called 'the Old Soldier'. They all fell over the guy ropes, punched the wrong man, and things looked as if they might turn ugly when one of them drew a bayonet.

"Fortunately, the Old Soldier, more than a match for any of his opponents singly, now had the sense to make himself scarce..."

I like to think that was him. As a barman he would have seen fights like this times without number in Ashington and along the Scotswood Road in Newcastle. I can see him winding up the young lads, without serious intent, but them taking it the wrong way. I can see him judging when to fight and when to run, and I think this would have got him through the entire war.

And I think that this partly explains why he entered the war as a private and left it at the same rank. If we can inherit qualities from our forebears (and we clearly can) then I can speak confidently on Geordie's behalf.

He would not want to be promoted, not even to Lance Corporal, because he would not want to give orders to his mates. He did what he had to do when he got his medals, but it wasn't because he wanted stripes, or advancement. It also gave him, in a strange way, a subtle kind of power over the endless stream of young new officers who came into the Battalion still yearning for glory. This lowly private G.M. Richardson was really a much-decorated 'Old Soldier' who had already achieved what they had dreamed about back in their public schools. They wouldn't quite know how to deal with him and – if they'd any sense – would have deferred to him in many secret ways.

What is striking about many of the personal accounts of the Great War is how, despite everything, there were many moments of great delight and fun, though I don't need to go into that here. As a Dad, looking at my grandad when he was of an age to be my son, I want to think it wasn't all unrelieved gloom. And certainly in the photograph, now re-dated by Graham Stewart's insight, there was still sparkle about him.

But it waz the same for me doon the pits, Alan.
Eh?
Ye mek it seem as if Ah waz some sort of victim. Ah had loadsa laughs.
But you were trapped.
Ah couldha left and got a job doon in London near Jack any time Ah wanted. Ah wazn't a dummy ye knaa.
But you stayed.
Ah had tae, tae look efter you and Pat. Yer Mam was…
You held the line Dad.
Oh divvn't start that again…

There are three details which have come down to us, his grandchildren, about Wor Geordie.

My cousin Shirley, who is the only one of us who knew him, remembers sitting on his lap as a little girl, in Ashington, and listening to the BBC radio with their cryptic broadcasts to the French Resistance: *The long sobs of the violins of Autumn* was one of them, and although no civilians knew it, it was the signal that the Invasion was under way and effectively said: 'Get started blowing up them bridges, Jacques!' She recalls that he was blind in one eye and had said that he was gassed at Hill 60.

And there is Dad's statement to me that the man had been injured in battle, but went back as a stretcher bearer. This might explain the newspaper reference to him: 'removing wounded men to safety while under heavy fire.'

Even so, I don't know if he came to serve as a stretcher bearer full time in the 13th Battalion, or if it was just an isolated piece of rescue work by him. Many of the stretcher bearers were conscientious objectors. Those countless numbers whose lives were saved by them spoke of them as being the bravest soldiers of all.

Not only were they getting shot at while doing their job, they also had the problem of dragging their feet out of the mud after every step, while making sure not to rock the stretcher as this would increase the pain of the wounded man. The pain of shattered bone ends grating together was so intense that the wounded man was likely to die of shock. One stretcher-bearer working in the mud in 1916 reported that: 'as one carried a wounded man you got stuck in the mud and staggered. You put out a hand to steady yourself, the earth gave way and you found you were clutching the blackened face of a half-buried, dead soldier.'[72]

They also tended wounded Germans.

The hard details about him are pretty much exhausted, I suspect. The fact that he won medals is impressive but – as he would be the first to insist – that doesn't elevate him one inch above the Geordies around who simply did their bit, as best they could. He was injured again in May 1918, and I'll wager that was when he

---

72 http://www.spartacus.schoolnet.co.uk/FWWstretcher.htm

lost the sight of his eye and finally 'copped a Blighty' to get sent home to Ashington.

I hoped he stayed there until the guns stopped on 11th November. I hope he was happy. He certainly created a lot more children: William, Doris, Isobella and Jack. And being a Territorial he got his old job back at the Grand Hotel which he kept for some years before working overground as a colliery screener in one of the mines. In truth, it no longer matters to me what he did in terms of soldiering because I can now acknowledge this:

He supported his family at home in Ashington as best he could by sending them money from his army pay. During the war he fought bravely in the battlefields of Flanders and took part in the most brutal and senseless battles in history, suffering hardships, horrors and loss that we in the 21st Century cannot begin to imagine, and never want to know. Somehow, despite being in the front lines where his mates were cut down on a daily basis, wading hip deep in corpses, amid the mud, rats, shells, exhaustion, gas attacks, bombing, disease and sheer unrelenting terror... somehow, that tough old bugger survived.

No, I never knew him. He died 7 years before I was born. But in the writing of this I have come to love him.

11

KEEPING WATCH

WHERE am I now?
I'm standing at the Grand Corner in Ashington, leaning on the railings which weren't there in Wor Geordie's day, but which my Dad used to lean upon and chat to his cronies. There is a side of my brain which is holding onto the same metal and saying: *I'm sorry Dad. I did my best too* – but I think he knows that, as Dads do.

Mam died of colonic cancer in 1985 after a long illness. In her last weeks she discharged herself from hospital. Dad became her full time carer, getting up many times in the night to take her back and forth to the toilet, helping her with all sorts of intimate nursing things. He treated her beautifully, as he always tried to. This time, having stopped demonising him, she let herself see.

"Ah've got meself a good 'un here!" she crowed to anyone who would listen. Meaning my Dad of course. The venom had ended. Everything he did was right. Everything he said was interesting. She stopped trying to shoot him down. She loved him again.

He always was *a good 'un* thought me and my sister, gritting our teeth and almost wanting to scream it at her out loud.

As I remember this my hands squeeze the cold metal of the railings and the knuckles turn white, but I search for my own armistice these days, and look to Dad's example.

Gazing north, the pit heaps are all gone along with the collieries, and it seems that there is a fourth road going across where those Ashington Alps used to lie. A statue of Jackie Milburn graces the now pedestrianised main street, and while there are a still a thousand lads dreaming of football glory, you'd be lucky to find a working miner anywhere.

Yesterday, on August 22nd and what would have been Dad's birthday, I stood at his grave with my sister Pat, who knew him infinitely better than I did. He adored her (as do I), but didn't know quite what to make of me. She told me that Dad, knowing he wouldn't see much of 1991, insisted he be buried in the double (unmarked) grave next to our grandfather. At least the distance that hung between them in life was put right after his death. Perhaps this book will do something to assuage his guilt about never really talking to his own Dad, or asking him about the Great War.

To my shame, I didn't know grandad had been buried there but I intend to give him a gravestone too. If they both bear the same name and bewilder the vicar then that's too bad, because they *still* won't get designated George Matthew Richardson Snr and George Matthew Richardson Jr. They are their own selves, and I hope they're cracking away in their mutual Geordie Heaven.

And what am I?

I now have a sort of Attestation Card of my own, as grandad had when he joined up, but these days it's called a Bus Pass, and it is proof that I too have become a silver-haired gadgy. Like him, my mind is filled with Flanders and I can't wait for some 21st Century Ashington youth to brush against me so that I can say 'Sand Fairy Anne bonny lad' though I might get my teeth bashed in if I do. If they no longer play tiggy with hatchets here, it's probably because they use tasers now.

I was initially going to finish by giving a list of the major battles fought by our Geordie's two battalions during the Great War, but the continuous warfare and incessant slaughter is just too much. I was also going to outline the Ludendorff Offensive in 1918 which – almost – smashed us to bits and achieved the longed-for breakout to the coastal ports but which instead ... petered out. I could have gone on to describe the Hundred Days Offensive which we launched in retaliation, leading to the collapse of the Hindenburg Line, the capitulation of the German Empire and the Treaty of Versailles which immediately sowed the seeds for World War 2.

But none of it is derring do or Boys Own adventuring, and you feel as sorry for the Germans caught up in it all as you do for our own lads and you just want to turn your eyes away after yet another massacre.

Mainly, I wanted the avatar I created help me glimpse the Great War through different eyes, and I think I've done that for my own purposes at least. Readers out there are quite welcome to use Wor Geordie to go marching on wherever they want to take him.

But I wasn't quite finished. It was that vicar's fault again. The one who pitched me the lines: *pit lie idle, pit lie idle,* and started something thrumming.

Again, very late at night, I went and re-read that book of his which I had downloaded: *When the Lantern of Hope Burned Low*, by the Reverend R. Wilfrid Callin, which is available free on various sites. It's subtitled: *The Story of the 4th Battalion Northumberland Fusiliers (T.F.) during the German Offensives of March, April, May 1918.*

Robert Graves created the stereotype of the Roman Catholic priest going into No Man's Land to tend to the wounded while the Church of England vicar stayed well away from anything upsetting. Totally wrong as far as this padre was concerned. Our Reverend Wilfrid, a Manxman, was in the thick of it, and when he penned his short and rather beautiful book there is blood and his tears on every page because he clearly adored the men he ministered to.

As he wrote his memoir, late at night in his Lincolnshire vicarage, less than a year after the war had ended, his nostrils still tingled with the memory of the gas. He could still hear, in his words, the ugly zipp-zipp of the bullets and the crash of falling shells and remember the terrifying sight of the grey hordes of Germans pouring on, pouring on toward them, with the sun glinting off the bare steel of the bayonets.

As he wrote on the very first page about his Battalion at that time of the Ludendorff Offensive:

> Three times in less than ten weeks we met the full shock of the enemy's strongest blows; three times by an inscrutable Fate we were at the very centre of his deadly attack. We do not complain, neither do we boast; in life and death we did but our duty; but in the dying of our indomitables is written the whole spirit of a great deliverance. We were of Britain, and Britain was at bay; that was all.

'We were of Britain, and Britain was at bay; that was all.' That was all…

Ye gods but I would follow a vicar like that. I would take his wafers and drink his wine and go to his church fêtes and be a good parishioner and organise Bingo after communion and try hard to believe. I can see him as he writes, stopping to dip his pen in the inkwell, stopping to dry his tears with the handkerchief he keeps on the desk next to his left hand.

He provides photographs of the men, and even the regimental goat, as a way of creating his own Necronomicon – or Book of Dead Names. He describes how, as the battle moved steadily through Harbonnières, Guillaucourt, and Ignacourt to effect an undramatic but highly important rearguard action which covered the retirement of the main body, he became aware of the plight of the refugees, tramping slowly west along the roads.

> With household goods piled high on barrows and trucks, elderly men and women trudged drearily on. Gone was the light from their faces, gone the music from their speech. Tears and despair ruled them. Sometimes, from sheer weariness they would drop by the roadside, as deaf to the shelling as the most hardened veteran. As for the children, clinging to their mothers skirts or lending their puny strength to push the barrow on which was their little all, the sight of them would have broken any heart but that of a German. In these circumstances Thomas Atkins betrayed those tender traits which have won for ever the heart of the peasantry of France. With no thought of his own tiredness, or yet of his own weighty kit he cracked a joke in the broad Northumberland accent, and put his shoulder to the wheel. Thus they lived, fought, laughed, and sometimes died.

The Northumberland Fusiliers were exhausted but he saw them contest every mile of ground, holding on to the last moment, counter-attacking when hopelessly outnumbered and thus robbing the Germans of their vital *elan*, making them hesitate, and contributing a full quota to the fighting which robbed the enemy of the prize for which he strove so much. The Germans were never going to reach the coast and the all-important ports if these battered, shattered battalions of the Northumberland Fusiliers had anything to do with it. "The rearguard action of the Fourth, a little thing in the mighty movements of these days, has yet in it that fire and glory which make such things historic."

He has no love for the Germans, this vicar, and there are times when he seems to want to pick up a Lewis Gun himself and help the lads out. Perhaps he did. These were men he had lived with, laughed with, slept with in their trenches. And they fought – and continued to fight – because these ordinary yet extraordinary men believed in their cause and wanted to finish the job they started, so that we could all sleep safely in our beds at home.

And his final words, after many more miles of agony and utter admiration for the men with whom he marched, sums up all the things I wondered about at the beginning of this book. In his eyes these Geordies were:

> Men with the years and the faults of boys, men who scorned not to give Youth's flower and beauty to the dust, for us today. They sleep today by field and hedgerow, in ruined gardens and unlovely woods. Scarce one of them is marked. But if there be in war any greatness, any glory, it is theirs and theirs alone. With the supreme test thrust upon them, they met it with the supreme sacrifice. They held the foe, denied him the prize, until the last dark hour had passed and the sun of Victory and Peace came up "like thunder" upon an astonished world.
>
> Living! Salute the dead!

And I have to say, sitting here in the 21st Century, in a little flat in the heart of Wiltshire, I sit up straight with a lump in my throat and do exactly that.

So who am I now, finally?

I realise, with some surprise, that I am standing in a trench and have become that young officer I regularly saw in the False Memory I described much earlier, looking at his pocket watch and waiting to go over the top. *Tick tock tick tick...*

My uniform is clean and comfortable. My officer's cap fits perfectly. The puttees are done just-so and my boots sparkle. The trench is dry and well-built, there is no mud beneath the duckboards or on me. It's not that I've become anyone special, but maybe I've just allowed myself a little promotion. All the Dads are One Dad and the two young Geordies who spawned me have become like my sons. As an officer I want to do my best for them, and get us all home safe.

Thanks to Cousin Bill I have the medals and Geordie's old medal ribbons next to Dad's watch and I feel complete. The loss of several miles of colon was a small price to pay in terms of the time the convalescence bought me, which enabled me to research and write all this.

Haddaway ye big softie. Ah had worse than that doon the pit..
I'm sure you did Dad.
An' Ah had worse than both o' ye at Wipers!
Eh?
Eh?
Dad?!
Grandad?!!

In brief – and all thanks to General Haig – Cousin Bill now has a history and a family tree on the Richardson side going right back to 1841. He is in touch with all of his many scattered cousins and we plan to meet up next year. He is also taking lessons in Geordie as fast as I can send them and has a DVD called *Ashington, Biggest Mining Village in the World* which shows the mines and the pit heaps and the Grand Hotel where our Geordie Richison, fiddling aboot in the turret with Jinny Yellowley, started us all.[73]

What was that motto of the Northumberland Fusiliers? *Quo Fata Vocant* – 'Whither the Fates call'? Maybe we've been marching to their step throughout.

So all of the gears of Dad's Watch are turning and churning, ticking and tocking exactly as they meant to do. I'll make sure it's never over-wound, and that no-one will ever get near the jewels to remove them.

When I started this book I noted that while it was to be called *Geordie's War*, it could also be *Geordies' War*, because we're not all that different, no matter where we live or what rank we might seem to have.

And by the same token *Dad's Watch* could also be *Dads' Watch*, in the sense that there all those moments in a Dad's life when he has to keep watch over house and home, keep it safe, do his duty, watch out for anything that might creep across from No Man's Land to hurt his family in the night. So I reckon that every man jack of us – or rather, every man dad of us – has a similar watch tucked away in a little pocket or purse somewhere.

---

73 The plethora of Williams and Georges down through the generations can be so bewildering I've put a basic family tree at the end of this book. Any other lost relatives are more than welcome to contact me.

I realise that I have spent a long time in trenches of my own, and I think we all do. For years I have projected my own prejudices, presumptions and sheer bloody ignorance into the Great War of history and my own inner conflicts, firing these over No Man's Land like those bombs from the trench mortars – and often getting the stalks blasted right back at me after they exploded.

Like those poor wretches in the battle before St Eloi these slits in the ground are sometimes so narrow that every time someone moves the shit is slopped from side to side, back and forward through the generations, grandfather to son to grandson.

That can stop now. The cannons are silent and the earth is still. The sky above the trench is a clear blue. The mud is gone. I can hear the watch ticking away. There is a firm ladder next to me and I am not afraid of what I might find when I go over the top.

BOOKS TO READ

Tyneside Scottish — Graham Stewart & John Sheen (Pen & Sword)
Through German Eyes — Christopher Duffy (Phoenix)
1914-1918 — Lyn Macdonald (Penguin)
The Great War Handbook — Geoff Bridger (Pen & Sword)
Tommy — Richard Holmes (HarperCollins)
Ypres 1917 — Norman Gladden (Wm. Kimber)
The Northumberland Fusiliers — Walter Wood (London 1866)
The Unknown Soldier — Neil Hanson (Corgi)
The Fifth in the Great War — H.R. Sandilands (N&M Press)
Passchendaele — Nigel Steel & Peter Hart (Cassell & Co)
To End All Wars — Adam Hochschild (Macmillan)
Somme — Martin Gilbert (London 2006)
Sex and Light — Alan Richardson (Twin Eagle)
Shimmying Hips — Alan Richardson (Kindle)
Dark Light — Alan Richardson (Mutus Liber)

That third-to-last book, originally called *The Google Tantra*, has absolutely nothing whatsoever to do with the Great War but as it's my autobiography and Ashington and the Great Mother figure largely, I think you should all buy it.

The penultimate book is my legendary Lost Novel (it was under the bed for 30 years!) and is all about Newcastle United and the England team in the late 1930s, as told by the mistress of one of the players.

The final book, subtitled *A neo-Templar Time Storm*, is my newest, and is probably the greatest novel ever written about the Wiltshire Mobile Library Service – if only because it's the only novel ever written about the Wiltshire Mobile Library Service. My own magnificent Library Van plays a major part, but I'm afraid to let my bosses know about it.

APPENDIX 1

Northumberland Fusiliers Battle Honours

Battle honours are given to selected military units as official acknowledgement for their achievements. The list below is not complete.

Mons	Flers-Courcelette	Lys
Le Cateau	Morval	Estaires
Retreat from Mons	Thiepval	Hazebrouck
Marne 1914	Le Transloy	Bailleuil
Aisne, 1914,'18	Ancre, 1916	Kemmel
La Basée 1914	Arras, 1917, '18	Scharpenberg
Messines 1914, '17, '18	Scarpe, 1917, '18	Dracourt-Quéant
Ypres 1914, '15, '17, '18	Arleux	Hindenburg Line
Gravenstafel	Pilckem	Epéhy
St. Julien	Langemarck, 1917	Canal du Nord
Frezenburg	Menin Road	Beaurevoir
Bellewaarde	Broodseinde	Courtrai
Loos	Passchendaele	Selle
Somme, 1916, '18	Cambrai, 1917	Valenciennes
Albert, 1915, '16	St. Quentin	Sambre
Bazentin	Bapaume, 1918	
Delville Wood	Rosières	

APPENDIX 2

From the 1901 CENSUS

Living at 40 Rendell Street, Elswick:

Thomas Richardson	Hydraulic Craneman
Sarah Ann	
James Gilbert	Blacksmith
Ada	
George Matthew	Machinist
Thomas	Apprentice Ordnance Works
William	Bookshop Errand Boy
Joseph	

(*William went to America and fought for US Army in WW1*)

So...

George Matthew was born in Newcastle off the Scotswood Road in 1882. He was living as a boarder with Sam and Margaret Hart, at 3 Second Avenue, Ashington, while working as a barman at the Grand Hotel. For some reason he knocked 3 years off his age at the time of his marriage, at the age of 30.

Jane was born in Tritlington in 1888. At the time of the 1911 Census she was living in the home of Joseph and Ellen Wardle at 14 Myrtle Street. She gave her occupation as General Servant/Domestic, and in fact she was working at the same hotel.

Which brings us down to Wor Geordie's dynasty, which reads as follows:

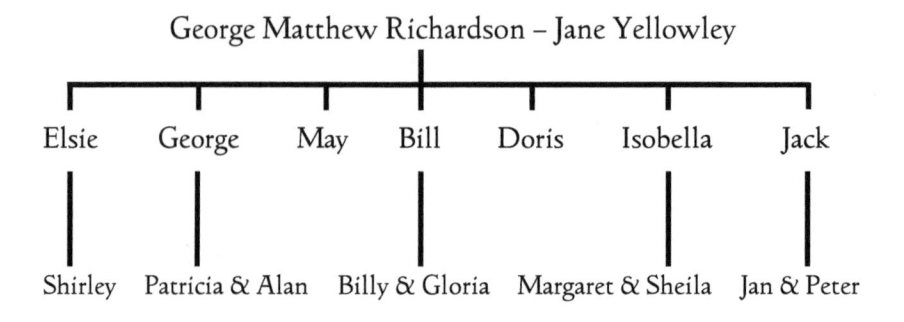

George Matthew Richardson – Jane Yellowley

Elsie	George	May	Bill	Doris	Isobella	Jack
Shirley	Patricia & Alan		Billy & Gloria		Margaret & Sheila	Jan & Peter

APPENDIX 3

My ultimate ancestor, as far as I have been able to track him back, came from...
Sunderland.

Lightning Source UK Ltd.
Milton Keynes UK
UKHW041441201218
334321UK00001B/127/P